"Reading *Leaving Silen[ce]* survivors through in-de[...] sexual survivors. A Go[d...] forward with accountabilmay to the church in all these situations and a strong call to move from silence to responsibility and accountability. Every church leader should have this book in their possession and read it diligently."

—**JO ANNE LYON**, general superintendent emerita of The Wesleyan Church

"*Leaving Silence* explores God's heart for the harmed, how we all can come to care for and empathize with the silenced, and why it matters. Susannah Larry invites all of us to center the narrative of the oppressed rather than the oppressor as we seek restoration and wholeness."

—**TIFFANY BLUHM**, author of *Prey Tell: Why We Silence Women Who Tell the Truth and How Everyone Can Speak Up*

"In *Leaving Silence*, Susannah Larry grapples with sexualized violence in Scripture and in the church, concepts of power and privilege, the role of family, and God's place in all of it. Her honesty and questions are refreshing. Her writing is clear and crisp. Larry does not sugarcoat the difficulty we find in the Scriptures. Nor does she gloss over the horrific. She unflinchingly looks evil in the face—and tells the truth—while standing with survivors, and demonstrates that our loving God is nothing like the corruption so many of us have experienced. This book is timely, needed, a gift. Every church should have a copy."

—**MARLENA GRAVES**, author of *The Way Up Is Down: Becoming Yourself by Forgetting Yourself*

"A profoundly caring book for anybody wrestling with biblical texts on sexualized violence. Writing from a deeply personal perspective of Christian faith, Susannah Larry considers biblical rape prose and poetry, including the story of Jesus, in light of contemporary and theological issues, among them consent, abuse of power, trauma, forgiveness, reconciliation, theodicy, evil, and God's love. The conversational and accessible tone of the reflections always supports victim survivors and the notion of a loving God."

—**SUSANNE SCHOLZ**, professor of Old Testament at Southern Methodist University Perkins School of Theology

LEAVING

SILENCE

Susannah Larry

Foreword by **KAT ARMAS**

LEAVING SILENCE

*Sexualized Violence, the Bible,
and Standing with Survivors*

HERALD
P R E S S

Harrisonburg, Virginia

Herald Press
PO Box 866, Harrisonburg, Virginia 22803
www.HeraldPress.com

Study guides are available for many Herald Press titles at www.HeraldPress.com.

LEAVING SILENCE
© 2021 by Herald Press, Harrisonburg, Virginia 22803. 800-245-7894.
    All rights reserved.
Library of Congress Control Number: 2021936517
International Standard Book Number: 978-1-5138-0817-8 (paperback);
    978-1-5138-0818-5 (hardcover); 978-1-5138-0819-2 (ebook)
Printed in United States of America

25 24 23 22 21   10 9 8 7 6 5 4 3 2 1

Dedicated to my three beautiful daughters,
Deborah, Gabrielle, and Carissa.

Every word I have written has been a prayer for your future.

CONTENTS

FOREWORD

In my early years as an evangelical after making the transition from Catholicism, I often found myself struck by the theological gymnastics many of my pastors and professors performed to try to explain the *why* behind many seemingly questionable things in the Bible. One such *why* concerned the story of Noah and why God would destroy the earth—and most of the people and animals on it—through a catastrophic flood.

We are told only that things became progressively evil and God regretted making humankind, deciding to start over by blotting out every living creature. Genesis 6 doesn't make it very clear what, exactly, is going on, introducing to the biblical narrative the presence of giants and divine beings that roamed the earth.

The reasoning I heard time and time again was that the corruption referred to the relations these divine beings and human daughters were having with one another. Not much more was said on the subject, and because the Bible felt so out of touch to me because of the theological gymnastics and lack of deep engagement with its difficulties, I didn't ask too many questions.

And then years later, after I graduated from seminary, #MeToo and #ChurchToo happened, and suddenly so many things that I had never really questioned in Scripture began to scream out at me from the pages of this sacred book. One day, I reread Genesis 6 and something peculiar caught my eye: "The sons of God saw that the daughters of humans were beautiful, and they married any of them they chose" (v. 2 NIV).

For the first time the thought crossed my mind: Perhaps it was this that made God regret making humankind: *that men (some sort of divine being, apparently) had objectified and taken women for themselves—whomever they chose—seemingly without their consent. Perhaps that was enough to make God want to start over.*

I don't know for sure if the corruption and violence that made God regret creating human beings on the earth was indeed the sons of God taking whatever women they chose. But noticing this detail sparked a new leg in my journey of discovery and asking the hard and uncomfortable questions when it comes to sexualized violence and the Bible.

Perhaps many people today are wary of Scripture because we've been told to love God with all our heart, mind, soul, and strength while simultaneously being expected to disengage from these very same things when reading Scripture. In evangelical circles, many of us were trained to zip right through stories of sexualized violence without much emotion or questioning—without a real wrestling—of the text. But loving God with our heart, mind, soul, and strength requires us to bring *everything* to the table—particularly our doubts, questions, disagreements, fears, frustrations, and even our traumas.

And this is precisely what Susannah Larry invites readers to do in this powerful and important work. Through her brilliant exegesis, Larry encourages us to engage *every part of ourselves*, reminding us that God hates sexualized violence enough to do drastic things—like give up divine privilege and hang naked on a cross—in full solidarity, understanding and identifying with our deepest pain.

As Larry so brilliantly points out, *Jesus is a survivor too.*

Within the pages of *Leaving Silence*, Larry offers us hope by presenting Scripture through a fresh and new lens for survivors of sexualized violence, those affected by it, and allies—reminding us that none of us are alone in our struggle.

Leaving Silence reminds us that the Bible is a nuanced account of the outworking of life, faith, and the human experience. It doesn't shy away from stories and questions thereof that are real and raw, and neither should we.

—Kat Armas
Author of *Abuelita Faith* and host
of *The Protagonistas* podcast

ACKNOWLEDGMENTS

A book like *Leaving Silence* takes shape in community. My community is broad and deep, and the influence and care of many individuals, churches, schools, and other institutions has brought me to this point of publication.

I would like to thank the team at Herald Press for their tireless work on my project and encouragement in its value. Dayna Olson-Getty invited me to submit my proposal at a time when doing so probably would not have occurred to me. Amy Gingerich's keen insight and emotional intelligence gave leadership to the project and shaped me as a first-time author. Meghan Florian's work as editor and consistent presence throughout the process made the workflow smooth and comprehensible. The marketing team's efforts to promote the book have meant that it will reach readers that, left to my own introverted devices, it never otherwise would have.

Rachel Martens's full review of the book represented the first time anyone had read this project from start to finish. Rachel's gift for theological and socially conscious discernment challenged me in many spots of my manuscript and encouraged me to refine my writing while also giving me the confidence that I had valuable chapters to share with the world.

My professors at Furman University and Vanderbilt University, no matter how many years ago I studied with them, are meaningfully present in this work. From Furman University, I would especially like to thank Roger Sneed, David Gandolfo, Claude Stulting, Shelly Matthews, and John Shelley, for their insistence on theological thinking that brought together academic concepts and real-life situations. Echol Nix taught my first course on liberation theology. As I mourn his passing, his memory is a blessing to me.

From Vanderbilt University, I would especially like to thank Annalisa Azzoni for the mentoring that got me through my PhD program and introduced me to feminist criticism of the Bible, including study of "texts of terror" within it. Choon-Leong Seow, my advisor, provided an insistence on scholarly excellence that continually pushed me to broaden my perspective. Herbert Marbury's classes on the Prophets and the Song of Songs profoundly influenced my understandings of sexuality in the Bible.

The schools where I have had the privilege of teaching have offered me faculty and students with whom to develop my ideas and test them in the classroom. I owe major thanks to Vanderbilt Divinity School and the School of Theology at Sewanee: The University of the South for allowing a PhD candidate to have the golden opportunity to teach your wonderful students. I am especially thankful for the support of my current institution, Anabaptist Mennonite Biblical Seminary, led inspirationally by David Boshart and Beverly Lapp, for its relational, scholastic, and institutional support during this season of my life. I have the most welcoming and supportive colleagues that anyone could ask for.

To the students I have taught: Your courage to look at hard texts and ask the important questions, all while vulnerably sharing parts of your lives, inspires my work here. Thank you for being in conversation with me. A special thank you to Sister Hannah at Sewanee, whose witness inspired me through this writing.

To the father of my children, and a partner who saw me through many of the days of writing this book, Will: Your constant support and belief in this project has made it flourish. Thank you for the conversations and time we shared together, as well as the vulnerability into your own journey, that helped me become the author of this book.

To those who were my classmates at Vanderbilt Divinity School: The conversations and support from so many of you brought me to many of the insights I share here. I was blessed to be part of such a pastorally and intellectually gifted cohort. Special thanks to my Korean brothers Seonwoong Hwang and Seonghyun Choi for being my "fictive kin" in the library and Bible classes and still seven years after graduation.

To the community of Hively Avenue Mennonite Church, my current congregational home: Thank you for giving me opportunities to lead from a place of authenticity and vulnerability. Thank you for supporting me in prayer and with tangible acts of love. I am so grateful for the family you have given me in northern Indiana. Special thanks to Elya and Jake Hess and their sons for allowing their home to be a place of sanctuary during the time of my writing.

My daughters, Debbie, Gabby, and Rissa, are too young to understand much about my book. However, I am most of all thankful to each of you. You inspire me to become a strong and kind woman who is worthy of your emulation. You give me courage to put my voice in the world.

All glory to God.

BEGINNING
THE JOURNEY

#METOO, THE FIRST TIME

I remember the day #MeToo started to go viral in 2017, while I was still in grad school. Scrolling mindlessly through Facebook while procrastinating on grading papers, I saw some of my friends posting their stories of sexual harassment and assault with the hashtag, or just #MeToo all by itself. My response was immediate and guttural. "#MeToo," I quickly typed, and clicked "post" before thinking too hard. My friends reacted with a mix of "likes," sad emojis, and hearts. "I know somebody else who would say #MeToo as well," a good friend of mine commented under my status. His comment was well meaning, but at the same time ironic—*of course* he knew someone else who could say #MeToo. I don't know a woman who couldn't.

Later, I learned about the burgeoning #ChurchToo movement as well. One of my friends courageously posted a blog with the hashtag, narrating her own experience of sexualized violence in a church-related context. Unfortunately, the words of Scripture, even of Jesus himself, have often been twisted and abused to protect perpetrators of sexualized violence in our midst, who include church leaders themselves. Too often, when survivors come to church leaders and "confess" their trauma history, the first words spoken by these trusted spiritual mentors are an insistence on forgiveness. As I'll explore more later, this approach does more harm than good. The church bears the brokenness of sin in our world and cannot be exempt from the scrutiny we apply to other sectors of society.

When I typed #MeToo for the first time, I felt a power I'd never experienced previously. That's because #MeToo reminds me of Christmas Eve. In the Christmas Eve services I've attended, there's a moment in the worship experience when all the lights go out. You know other people are there, but you can't really see them clearly. Nor are you really seen. Then somebody lights their little candle off the Christ candle of the Advent wreath and passes the light to somebody else. The new light-bearer lights their neighbor's candle, and the neighbor lights the next. Before long, the whole church is full of dancing flames from the candles. The faces of your neighbors are illuminated in a beautiful, fiery glow. The flickering candlelight swallowed the solitude that reigned just a few moments earlier.

#MeToo and #ChurchToo have been a lot like that for many people I know. When you're a survivor, you *know* there are other people out there with a story like yours. But finding each other and standing together is hard when shame pushes you into the shadows. At its best, #MeToo is like that flame, which one person boldly first held aloft, that invites others to the light as well. As Jesus says, "In the same way, let your light shine before others, so that they may see your good works and give glory to your Father in heaven" (Matthew 5:16). Knowing that other lights are out there—and that shame couldn't put them out—gave me the courage to step into the light.

However, the #MeToo and #ChurchToo movements aren't perfect. Certain types of survivorship are more recognized than others. Straight white women's stories of power-based personal violence are more "seen" than any other group's narratives. The proliferation of #MeToo on social media can also create the impression that if you're a survivor, it's your *obligation* to tell your story. If you don't, you might be letting other survivors down. Or your pain might not be legitimate. Nothing could be further from the truth: The whole point of #MeToo should be that each survivor owns their own story, whatever that ownership means to them. Safety and wellness come first. While the pioneers of the movement didn't intend for any of these issues to arise, when something goes viral on social media, it takes on a life of its own.

I'm a seminary professor, responsible for teaching people preparing to go into ministry about sacred Scriptures. Because of this role, I'm honored to have conversations with survivors of sexualized violence on a regular basis. I've seen people come up against these limits of the #MeToo movement. I think there's no pain more piercing than an unacknowledged one. I am here to say: You don't have to fit into any kind of box to have suffered through sexualized violence. Your personal identifiers might be different from the ones that you see publicized in connection with the #MeToo movement. You don't need to have said "Me, too" to read this book and have a seat at this table. Your story is *your own*. You don't owe it to anyone. Your healing journey is your own, too. The strength and solidarity that I found through typing #MeToo might not be there for you.

As a matter of fact, I know from the conversations I've had that many survivors feel that God isn't there for them, either. People who regard me as an "expert" on the Bible often come to me with questions about God and Scripture. "Why does

God allow—or even encourage—violence in the Bible?" they ask me. "You told us you're a feminist—why do you think the Bible is authoritative?" Or sometimes, "Why do you love the Old Testament so much, even though it's so violent and out of step with the way of Jesus?" Or maybe, "My mother-in-law married another woman. I believe in gay rights and I certainly oppose violence against gay people . . . but I don't know how to be a faithful Christian at the same time. Can you help me?" Or "If women aren't responsible for the fall, why did the church treat me this way?"

I feel the weight of these questions heavily. They're real and important, and under them all, there's a bigger, underlying question: "How is the promise of God to be with us, to be *Emmanuel*, fulfilled through the words of the Bible?" My conviction is this: If God is the capital *G* God whom our Scriptures and tradition proclaim, then God is with us through the contexts that cause us to type #MeToo into the yawning maw of social media. God is with us—and *for* us—in moments of abuse and assault. God is with us when our stories are not believed. God is with us when we file a report, and when we do not. God is with us when a friend, family member, or trusted authority betrays us. The God who made us in his image and who molded us lovingly from dust with his hands is fighting a battle for justice alongside us, within us, and in ways that transcend our human understanding.

THIS BOOK IS FOR YOU

Usually, dedications appear in the front matter of a book, and if you check, there's one in my book as well. If you're like me, though, you'll often page past these dedications in a hurry to get to the real substance of what you're trying to read. In my book, the dedication is the whole reason for this book's existence, and it's simply too important for me to put it in a place that's easy to skip. The stories that have been shared with me have formed what I've written here. I believe these stories, and they have changed me, forming my heart into ways of compassion and justice that more closely mirror the God in whose image we have all been made. I am so grateful and honored to have received these stories. This book is my gift back to all those who have shared their stories with me, or who bravely are finding their way through life even though it's so difficult at times. So this book is for you.

This book is for you if you were abused as a child but are fuzzy on the details.

This book is for you if you're still angry and haven't forgiven those who have abused you.

This book is for you if you were drunk before an assault.

This book is for you if you changed your mind during a sexual act.

This book is for you if you were silent during an assault.

This book is for you if you don't fit the picture of "survivor" that most people imagine.

This book is for you if you chose not to report your abuse.

This book is for you if you'll *never* type #MeToo.

This book is for you if you're still in that abusive relationship.

This book is for you if no other person has believed you yet. (I do, by the way.)

This book is for you if you loved the person who hurt you.

This book is for you if an abuser's elevation to public office or another leadership position turns your stomach.

This book is for you if you're not sure what to call the thing that happened.

This book is for you if your only prayer is, "My God, why have you forsaken me?"

This book is for you if you're a loved one of a survivor.

This book is for you if you want to minister without doing more harm.

This book is for a generation of children who deserve less pain.

This book is for me, too.

GUIDEPOSTS

On any journey, you need signs to show you the way. If you have any traveling companions, it's also helpful to have some agreements about your trip that you hold in common. If you're going on this journey with me, I think it's only fair for you to know where my investments lie. Here are my guideposts for this book.

I believe that the Bible is the Word of God . . . but, in accord with many other Christians throughout history and the Bible itself, the Bible is not the *only* word of God. According to Scripture, at times the word of God is a *spoken* word, not a written one, revealed outside the pages of the Bible. As a Christian, I believe that Jesus Christ is the Word made flesh. For that reason, I'm wary of treating the Bible as an idol, as if it's the *only* way we know God's revelation to us.

There is no "literal" interpretation of Scripture. In certain circles of Christians, it's popular to claim that one is interpreting the Bible just as it was written, for example, considering Genesis 1–3 as a historical account of how the creation of the world and the "fall of man" happened. Three points are important here. First, a "literal" reading is just not possible. Unless you are an ancient person living in the regions in which the Bible was written and belong to the small group of people who were the intended audience, any act of reading the Bible you do will be an act of translation—linguistically and culturally. Second, a "literal" reading is not the only Christian way to read the Bible—nor is it necessarily the most "traditional" one. *From the very beginning of Christian interpretation*, there were always multiple schools of thought on how to read the Bible. Third, I believe that this approach to the Bible often does violence to the biblical text itself—the very text it claims to venerate! There's so much more to the Bible than just "historical accuracy"—and at the end of the day, I'm not sure historical accuracy is the most important thing. There are diverse genres within Scripture we can appreciate, complex and all-too-human characters, heartbreaking loss, and victorious gain. If we're too focused on finding what we think is a literal reading, we can fail to appreciate the full beauty, wisdom, and power that these texts offer us today.

I believe that, guided by the Holy Spirit, humans wrote the Bible. As people wrote the Bible, they were trying to bear witness about what God was doing in their lives and communities. Often, the results tell us much about the heart of God. At other times, the Spirit guides us to reject certain ideas or practices that the authors would have taken for granted. Yet even in these moments of pushback, I believe that God will be faithful to his promise not to allow his word to come back empty (Isaiah 55:11).

I believe that contemporary academic tools can help us draw closer to God through reading the Bible. The Bible doesn't "belong" to people who are experts in these methods, and I don't think that you need to know them for God to use the Bible to speak truth and wisdom to and through you. And yet—I think our intellectual capacities are gifts from God. Academic disciplines can serve the end of loving God with all we have and all we are—including with our minds (Matthew 22:37).

I believe we have to do the work to try to understand the Bible on its own terms—while not compromising ours. At the time the Bible was written, people understood their world in ways quite different from the ways we do today. For instance, as I'll discuss later, in the ancient Israelite society reflected in the Old Testament, women didn't really have much in the way of sexual agency. That makes defining "rape" in the Bible a tricky question. *Understanding* that reality makes the texts we'll talk about make more sense and helps us know where the authors were coming from—and yet that understanding doesn't justify people's actions in the passages we'll talk about.

I believe that your holistic well-being is more important than my book. In this book, I discuss issues of sexual violence in each chapter. If you are a survivor and currently experiencing active symptoms of trauma, this may not be the best book for you right now. You are not alone. You are worthy, loved, and believed. There are people in your community who can become trusted supporters on your journey to healing. Please consider putting down this book and finding yourself some support before you dig into the chapters, because the context I'll discuss will get painful and nitty-gritty at times. At the end of this book, I've included a list of organizations that may be resources to you. This book will still be here when you are ready.

I believe that sexualized violence is about power, not about sex. I prefer the term *sexualized violence* to *sexual violence*, simply because the best research from the social sciences suggests that what we think of as "sexual violence" isn't primarily sexual at all. Contrary to the popular (and false) myth, women aren't assaulted because they look too sexy—because that skirt was too short or that top was too low-cut. Men don't abuse young boys *because* they identify as gay. People don't *usually* become sexual predators because their lust is too uncontrollable.

No, the violence is usually about *power*. People's misguided and sinful desire to hold power over others, to overcome their own feelings of power*less*ness by exploiting others, can manifest itself in acts that wreck lives. Sometimes these types of behaviors appear sexual in nature. Are these inappropriate actions *about* sex, fundamentally? No. Yet they have to do with the way we express and understand ourselves as sexual beings. That's why I'll often use the term *sexualized violence*.

THE JOURNEY AHEAD

On a journey, you need not only guideposts, but also an idea of where you're headed. Oftentimes, it's the journey that shapes us as much as the destination . . . but having that destination in mind helps us have something to press toward. The road I take through this book reflects much of my own journey. The topics I chose are by no means the *only* approach one could take to consider sexual violence in the Bible and in the life of faith, and the route I've decided upon is shaped by the questions I'm asking and the questions that others have asked of me.

The journey begins with the realization that those of us who call ourselves Christian, who belong to the church, have a problem. It isn't just our problem, but it's one that we (collectively, as the church) have both contributed to and suffered from in the broader culture. The problem goes something like this: We worship a God whom we believe is all-loving, all-knowing, and all-powerful. Yet dehumanizing things of a sexualized nature happen to us, and God seems silent. Worse still, when we turn to the Bible for comfort, as many of us have been taught to do, the generalities of God's presence with us don't seem obvious when we read stories and other texts about sexualized violence. Usually, it seems that victims bear the blame, the pain, and the responsibility for fixing the situation. God doesn't seem to be on "our side" at all. If we turn to the church for help, our pain might be made worse. We might be told that whatever abuse we experienced was our fault. Our abusers might be protected. The abuser might even be a person of authority within the church.

All of these things seemingly counter the central idea of Christianity: That Jesus is Emmanuel, "God with us." A God who is with us—*really* with us—is with us when our souls groan, our bodies ache, and our minds are on fire from abuse. A God who is with us—*really* with us—will stand up for us even if no one else does. A God who is with us—*really* with us—will work for our healing and strive for our justice.

The question is, can we find a God like that witnessed to within the pages of Scripture? My answer to that question is an unapologetic yes. My destination, wending its way through difficult and often disturbing texts, is the idea that we can find a God who is *really* with us within the Bible.

The chapters I've written don't need to be read in order. While they move in a general trajectory, I invite you to jump in wherever the Spirit leads and go from there. Here's a quick overview of each of them so you can see where you might be interested in starting.

In chapter 1, I start out by considering what I consider an "original sin" in Genesis: that of power-based personal violence involving sexual coercion. I start with the story of Hagar in Genesis 16 and 21. For many Christians, Hagar isn't a household name like her owners' names are. But Hagar begins the Bible's story of God's attention to those who have been exploited by sexualized violence. Hagar is a slave who is handed over by her mistress, Sarah, to have sexual intercourse with Abraham, Sarah's husband (and Hagar's master), to serve Sarah's own reproductive goals. If that's not a case of sexualized violence, I'm not sure what is. Yet white Christian culture has often glossed over Hagar's suffering or read her story merely as one of faith and blessing. Still, God has not forgotten her. In this chapter, we'll take a look at how God does *not* turn a blind eye to sexualized violence that others overlook because of its intersections with inequality. God is the One Who Sees Us, our holy witness.

In chapter 2, we'll turn to two other stories that, in the history of biblical interpretation, have often been considered rape narratives, that of Dinah (Genesis 34) and Tamar (2 Samuel 13). We'll consider the stories of these women and notice some major differences between them. I point out how crucial survivors' testimonies are as we think about stories of sexualized violence. I also introduce the figure of Daughter Zion in Lamentations, who, representing the people of Judah, tells her own story of sexual assault alongside that of other women who have suffered under enemy conquest. The Bible invites us to own our own narratives of survivorship and decide whether and to whom to share our stories. Also in this chapter, I reflect more on what it means to be an ally to people who have experienced trauma, and share some things to keep in mind so we can truly stand in solidarity.

One of the biggest challenges of the current #MeToo cultural climate we're in—as empowering as it has been for many survivors—is that it's privileged certain types of stories over others. Some survivors have not felt that the option was there for them to tell their stories—regardless of whether this self-disclosure was one they wanted to make. As a professor working in a Christian seminary (where many people are working to come to terms with their identities as survivors) and as someone whose loved ones include male survivors, I recognize this privileging of certain stories as an unacceptable situation. So in chapter 3, I explore how the Bible opens the door for an understanding of men as survivors, as well. I take a look at Leviticus 18:22 and 20:13, which offer a window into how male-on-male sexual violence was used as a means of shaming men. This concept plays itself out in two other narrated scenarios of attempted gang rape of men found in Genesis 19 and Judges 19. And I think through how the story of Joseph and Potiphar's wife (Genesis 39) points to the precarious position of many men who may face power-based personal violence, as well as stop along the way with Samson, who withdraws his consent for sex acts.

Ideally, our family members and other loved ones would be the first ones at our side when we're affected by sexualized violence, but sadly, that often isn't the case. In chapter 4, I explore how the Bible enters into the complicated nexus of familial betrayal. At times, as in 2 Samuel 13, a family member is actually the perpetrator of the sexualized violence. Tragically, sexualized violence prompts family responses that are less than helpful and are often actively harmful. Sometimes, sexualized violence precipitates complete familial rejection. The graphic story of Judges 19–20 illustrates this scenario, as when a gang-raped daughter is shut out of her father's home after her assault.

Often, one of the major challenges that survivors face is the question of blame. In searching for a reason that the terrible event of sexualized violence could have happened to us, we often end up pointing a finger at ourselves. Sometimes, ironically, it's less painful to blame ourselves than the person who's actually responsible. Sometimes, our upbringing or inundation with a certain way of thinking may lead us to believe that if something bad happens to us, it must be our fault. Sometimes, we just want to have a reason for our own pain. In chapter 5, I take up the question of blame, using the book of Lamentations as a guide. Lamentations pushes back against the theology, present in much of the Bible, that suffering happens because a person sinned. In fact, the female speaker in Lamentations goes so far as to say that *even if we have "sinned"* (and who hasn't?) *and a traumatic sexual event came next*, the "sin" doesn't explain why someone harmed us. The "sin" doesn't justify it. We are *not* to blame. We have the right to be angry, hurt, and struggling.

At the center of Christianity is the idea that Jesus Christ became fully human, born to experience the entirety of our lives in this beautiful and broken world. He knows what it's really like to be us. Jesus' story intersects in many ways with sexualized violence, and in chapter 6 I consider how the unfolding of Jesus' life from conception to the ascension teaches us about this topic. Jesus' ministry in many ways teaches us about God's heart for survivors. But not only that, Jesus is a survivor. His death on the cross involved sexualized violence on the way as he was left naked to breathe his last. And for those of us who are survivors as well, I believe this can give us hope that God revealed in Jesus Christ understands our deepest pain.

Throughout the Old Testament and the New Testament, the overwhelming witness of the Bible is toward a God who sees and believes us when we declare, however tentatively, "Me, too." We are not alone. God sees us, believes us, and strives for our healing. After all, God is a survivor, too.

1

AN ORIGINAL SIN

*Sexualized Violence, Power,
and the God Who Sees*

IN THE BEGINNING

Sexualized violence starts in the beginning. Well, not quite
in the beginning: the good world that God creates in Genesis 1–2 does not include the horrors of violence that humans
would soon inflict on one another. That state of paradise may
not have lasted long, but it reveals God's deepest desires for
humanity to live in relationship with one another. Beloved
partners could behold each other naked and without shame.
Gendered hierarchies didn't exist. Creation was there to enjoy
and share, not to dominate and hoard.

But it didn't take long for violence to enter the world. The
first humans' decision to rival God resulted in their expulsion
from the garden. The same aspirations to power and control
that led Eve and Adam to taste the forbidden fruit lie at the
root (pun unintended) of sexualized violence. In the decision
to taste the fruit, the famous "first couple" aspired to be like
God, knowing good and evil. In this desire lies a thirst for
power that goes beyond the scope of how God created humans

to live in community together. God called us to be partners with one another, to care for our world together, and to enjoy the goodness that God freely offers us. Instead, we opted for coercive power over each other, to exploit the world, and to take what we want.

Sound familiar?

The power-grabbing implicit in sexualized violence should be no surprise to us. It's imbedded in our very first story. Some folks might take that to mean that we're just stuck with sexualized violence, making the case that if it's a result of the fall of humanity, it's now simply part of human nature.

Nothing could be further from what I mean to say in this chapter. As Christians, we believe in a God who, through Jesus Christ, is working for the renewal of all creation. Through the writings of both the Old Testament and the New Testament, we see a vision of creation restored to God's intention for it. Restoration of God's reality will look like a reality where all people enjoy and share the goodness of God's creation—which includes our bodies—together.

SIN BREAKS IN (GENESIS 16)

The sinfulness manifested in the fall keeps playing itself out in a new story fraught with sexualized violence, that of Sarah, Abraham, and Hagar.[1] In the telling of this story that I grew up with, and those with which I'm most familiar in the Christian tradition, Hagar does not figure majorly. Indeed, she's kind of the original third wheel in the grand narrative of God's faithfulness to Abraham playing out; Abraham and Sarah are the main participants in God's plan, but Hagar is at best a distraction.

Abraham and Sarah do not seem to be able to have children together—or, in the troublesome language of the Old

Testament, Sarah was "barren." I say "troublesome" because in the Old Testament worldview, male factor infertility was not understood as a possible reason for years of infertility like Abraham and Sarah experienced. God repeatedly promises Abraham endless offspring, but Abraham is not comforted. Sarah takes matters into her own hands and offers her slave to Abraham, as, essentially, a breeder. Sarah will get credit for the child's birth, and her status in the household will be reinforced as a mother—albeit through surrogacy—of Abraham's child. As it turns out, though, this scheming isn't necessary. God is faithful to his promise to continue Abraham's line through Sarah. And when this promise is fulfilled, Sarah and Abraham are quick to discard Hagar when her reproductive capacities and Ishmael, her son, are no longer needed.

WHOSE STORY?

In the story I just told, which is the one I grew up hearing, Hagar doesn't play much of a role. She is merely the uterine accessory of Abraham and Sarah, caught up in their bigger plans and covenant with God. In the Christian traditions I'm familiar with, the main problem noted in this entire scenario is Abraham and Sarah's lack of faith. They don't sufficiently trust in God's promises to them and wait for God's word to them to come true.

Faithlessness may indeed be a problem—but reading from my vantage point, the most devastating issue in this story is sexualized violence. I became cognizant of this manifestation of sexualized violence only after studying the work of womanist scholar Delores Williams, who in her germinal book *Sisters in the Wilderness* points out the many ways in which Hagar's experiences of loss of bodily autonomy and surrogacy on behalf of a more privileged woman echo the pain that enslaved women in America endured under the death-dealing system of chattel slavery, as well as later under Jim Crow. Biblical scholar Nyasha Junior has more recently written about Hagar's position within the Bible and interpretation. As a white woman who has benefited from privilege my whole life, I find it challenging to read Williams's and Junior's critiques. First of all, they illustrate how women like me participate in other women's oppression and entrench their experiences of sexualized violence. Intentionality or lack thereof does not absolve us of classism and racism. While I, as a woman, have experienced disadvantage, vulnerability, and even sometimes suffering because of my gender, I also have experienced unearned privilege because of my skin color. It's far too easy for me to look past Hagar because what she experiences falls so far outside my own experience. This is not the case for everyone.

It's easy to dismiss interpretations that don't line up with our own life experiences, or when the concerns addressed don't match the ones most pressing to us. However, I'm learning that when I encounter an interpretation I want to dismiss, it often means that the interpretation in question is pressing against the lines of power that I carry—and that I may even idolize. I need to take seriously the fact that for many African American women, Hagar, not Sarah, is the figure in the Genesis story with whom they relate. Hagar's disempowerment, forced surrogacy, and abuse reflect the roles that white supremacy still coerces Black women to fill today. The unfortunate fact is that I still participate in these systems of white supremacy. My blindness and inaction perpetuate systemic and personal harm across lines of race, class, and sexuality. When I'd like to reject interpretations that centralize Hagar and the problems that persist because of a legacy of slavery, my resistance is mainly coming from an unwillingness to see because of my own position of power.

SARAH: VICTIM AND VIOLATOR

One of the most difficult aspects of this text for me is that another woman, a woman of greater privilege than Hagar, engineers Hagar's victimization. This difficulty is one that I relate to as a white woman who can type #MeToo yet has also benefited from the oppression of people in racial minority groups in the United States. Sarah's story is very much one in which I can find myself easily reflected. Sarah willfully participates in another woman's experience of sexual assault. To begin with, she is holding Hagar as a slave. While this was likely a norm for the times in which the Scriptures were written, and while we can certainly draw a distinction between the transatlantic slave trade and slavery in the ancient world, I believe the idea that a human can own another human is still fundamentally wrong, whether that slavery happened thousands of years ago, two hundred years ago, or today.

Sarah hands over her slave for her husband to have sex with. At least as the Bible tells it, this idea comes from Sarah herself, not from Abraham (Genesis 16:2). As far as we know, Sarah did not seek consent from Hagar before doing this. Unfortunately, the idea of "consent" is a modern one, and our classification of rape relies heavily on this modern-day notion. So it's harder to pinpoint what rape means in the absence of an understanding of consent. However, my guess is that Sarah, as a woman, had an idea of what it felt like to live in a body that was not really her own. She understood what it was like to submit or futilely resist sexual contact. She knew, and she chose to victimize Hagar anyway.

Why would Sarah do this? On one level, the answer is practical and straightforward. She wanted a child to call her own to secure her place in Abraham's lineage. She wanted to make sure she would have a son to feed her and protect her after Abraham died (assuming she outlived Abraham, which ultimately she did not). She wanted to escape the cultural umbrage of being a "barren" woman.

I think the answer might go yet deeper, though. The pain that Sarah puts Hagar through is borne, in part, of her own experiences teetering on the verge of sexualized violence. In a story occurring not long before Hagar's in the Genesis narrative, Abraham and Sarah are sojourning in Egypt because of a famine in Canaan (Genesis 12). Abraham, worried for his own life, decides that it is necessary to pass Sarah off as his sister. As the Jewish Publication Society translation renders it, Abraham exclaims, "I know what a beautiful woman you are. If the Egyptians see you and think, 'She is his wife,' they will kill me and let you live. Please say that you are my sister, that it may go well with me because of you, and that I may remain alive thanks to you." In other words, Abraham knowingly endangers Sarah and sends her into the chambers of Pharaoh. Her rape is a real possibility. Abraham's motivations do not seem entirely survival-based, either; Abraham profits economically from the ruse. He emerges from Egypt a wealthy man, having become rich from the livestock, gold, and silver of the Egyptians. After YHWH afflicts Pharaoh and his household with plagues because of the endangered matriarch, Pharaoh reacts with righteous indignation toward Abraham and banishes him. In fact, he is so eager to see Abraham gone that he sends lavish gifts with him.

The narrative of Genesis does not tell us what happened to Sarah in Pharaoh's palace, whether she was ever called upon to enter Pharaoh's bed, willingly or unwillingly. Without her testimony (see chapter 2 in this book), we cannot know. However, the writers of Genesis have a vested interest in keeping Sarah the exclusive sexual partner of Abraham. Should she have been impregnated by Pharaoh, God's promise to Abraham, to make of him a great nation through Sarah, would have appeared null and void. There would have been no way to tell whose baby Sarah was carrying. Therefore, the text at least makes it appear that Sarah is "rescued" before she has intercourse with Pharaoh, willingly or unwillingly. (This pattern would also be repeated in Abraham's interactions with Abimelech, a local king, in Genesis 20, and would also rear its head generationally, as their son, Isaac, makes a similar wife/sister bait-and-switch with his own wife, Rebecca, in Genesis 26.)

I think this experience shaped Sarah's interactions with Hagar profoundly. Whether or not she was actually forced into unwanted intercourse with Pharaoh, Sarah received the deep hurt of learning that women's bodies could be useful commodities in the power plays of men. She observed her husband using her body as a ploy to save his own life and even gain economically. While Genesis doesn't give any indication about Sarah's emotions during this time, I imagine that they would have been ones of fear, deep hurt, and confusion.

These are absolutely valid emotions. Sarah's wounding in this way was not her fault. Yet her trauma played out in behaviors for which she actually did bear much responsibility. As the saying goes, "Hurt people hurt people." Hagar, in the wilderness, would go on to receive a life-changing revelation from God that ultimately removed her from the situation in which she found herself. Sarah cannot claim the assurance that Hagar does, that God still sees her even and especially amid her most painful suffering. Certainly, at the very least, the theophany (appearance of God) that Hagar beholds is articulated more explicitly in the Genesis story.

God's actions on Sarah's behalf are trickier to identify, but they are there, more subtly. When she is in danger and the promises that God has made to Abraham are at stake, God does intervene. God sends plagues to Egypt, and Pharaoh realizes that the issue is the new addition to his harem. (We might ask why God doesn't choose to send plagues to Abraham instead, since it was Abraham's decision that placed Sarah inside the palace to begin with.) It is not Abraham's change of heart or Pharaoh's initiative that accomplishes Sarah's freedom, but God's intervention on her behalf.

God's action on Sarah's behalf, though often unnoticed, may speak to us in our circumstances as well. God is still working, even when God does not speak to us directly. God is still working, even when the deliverance comes in a different way than we might have expected. God's actions sometimes appear one or two times removed from us, and that can make it hard to relate our experience of suffering and its abatement to something that God is doing in the world.

Having an ally beside us in traumatic situations can play a huge role in how that experience of trauma shapes us. When we go through trauma, the times when we believe that we are not alone in the situation—even when the situation is really bad—turn out to be less traumatic than the situations in which we feel abandoned. Having allies alongside us builds our own resiliency, and their absence or perceived absence, through no fault of our own, intensifies the trauma of an already traumatic situation.

Being alone through trauma teaches us something: That we have to fight our battles alone. Sometimes, it teaches us that we have to look out for number 1 (ourselves) at any cost, because no one else will be there for us, no matter how much trouble we're in. If no further healing occurs in our lives, that knowledge of solitary trauma can harden us, at least on the exterior. No matter how broken or vulnerable we feel on the inside, we may try to protect ourselves by hardening our exterior to the point that we become unable to express empathy for others.

Survivors of abuse are not at all doomed to repeat the sins that have been visited upon them. However, I do think that the most painful parts of our pasts—parts that we haven't started to heal from—can hurt us and others when we least expect it. It's incredibly unfair. (And yeah, we all know that life isn't fair . . . but that type of unfairness was never part of God's vision for creation.) Sexualized violence wounds us, and then we have to pick up the pieces of ourselves so we don't wound others too. We are doing work that never should have been ours to do, while very frequently, the one who wounded us still doesn't realize they did anything wrong. Metabolizing our trauma is the only way to get our lives back and create new life around us instead of more brokenness. We should never have to bear this burden alone.

But Sarah believed that she was alone, and she wanted to see another woman humiliated. She wanted to see a woman brought down to a lower level than the one she occupied as a concubine in Pharaoh's palace or as a barren wife. Just as her body and its infertility had become her most defining feature, so she wanted to define and circumscribe another woman based on the same limiting criteria. Of course, none of these ideas would likely have entered Sarah's explicit thought process.

What if Sarah could have reframed her trauma to see God as a witness with her? True enough, God doesn't speak with Sarah directly in the way that Hagar received divine communication. However, through divine intervention, Sarah is delivered from potential threat because God sends a plague to Pharaoh's house. In the next episode where Abraham passes off Sarah as his sister (Genesis 20), God speaks directly to

Abimelech in a dream and warns him that Sarah is actually Abraham's wife. (Goodness, doesn't it seem like God talks to everyone *except* Sarah in these stories?)

I'm not wholly satisfied with how God responds. I wish God had spoken with Sarah and expressed that she was precious, chosen, and beloved. I think that she deserved to hear from God that what she'd experienced was wrong. Nevertheless, even though the story doesn't go the way I wish it would, there are ways that God is still acting as an advocate for Sarah.

It isn't Sarah's fault that she can't perceive the ways God is working on her behalf. Instead, the problem is that the people around her aren't communicating with her. What if Abraham had shared his conversation with Pharaoh? What if Abimelech's dream had been passed along to Sarah? We can't be sure, but I bet Sarah might have been in a different emotional place if she'd heard these details. What if Sarah had refused to put Hagar in the position of surrogacy?

These stories can teach us that we, too, might be able to trace ways where God was working on our behalf, even if the acts of God were not as apparent to us as they could have been.

HAGAR: A STORY OF RESILIENCE (GENESIS 16 AND 21)

God's presence as the one who sees us matters deeply. I see it mattering in the story of Hagar. Hagar encounters God when she has reached the bottom of the barrel—literally—as she, pregnant with Ishmael, is dying in the wilderness. She has fled a situation where she was forced into sex that would impregnate her and cause her to bear a child for another woman. The abusiveness of her situation magnified to include physical abuse as well. Once she has become pregnant, her owner Sarah "becomes light in her eyes" (Gen. 16:5) In other words, miraculously, Hagar has claimed her dignity and empowered herself in ways her owners did not anticipate. To use the language of white supremacy, she had become an "uppity" woman. It was then that Sarah began to "abuse" Hagar. The root here, *'innah*, matches the word that is often used in the cases in the Old Testament that have to do with rape. This word has a broader range of meaning to describe situations in which someone's personhood is being degraded (e.g., the slavery of the Israelites in Egypt). Now, I don't think that Sarah was necessarily abusing Hagar in a sexualized way. However, I do think the appearance of this word here suggests that the situation had *already* become one of sexualized violence because Hagar was forced to endure intercourse with Abraham. The sexualized violence entrenched even more deeply the power differential that already existed between Hagar and her owners. Everything that follows is tainted through the lens of this abuse.

I wish that God had descended in a blaze of glory and freed Hagar outright with a mighty hand and an outstretched arm. I wish that I could say that the angel of the Lord demanded, "Let my daughter go!" to Abraham and Sarah in the same way that Moses and Aaron faced Pharaoh. Unfortunately, that's not what happened. When Hagar cannot take the abuse anymore, she takes matters into her own hands. She flees into the wilderness while pregnant with her son, Ishmael.

Hagar makes a bold choice to lay claim to her motherhood of Ishmael, despite all the circumstances and injustices surrounding his birth. Perhaps this is part of the "uppity-ness" that Sarah finds so offensive. Hagar is meant to be trodden into submission, her strength, character, and witness squeezed out of her like toothpaste from a rolled-up tube. She does not comply. She fulfills the role of mother in her own way and on her own terms.

So when the situation boils over for Hagar, and what was already a coercive, sexually abusive environment adds a layer of physical abuse as well, Hagar leaves, carrying her unborn child. She has bigger dreams for her son than to grow up in a household where his mother is abused as a slave.

Hagar's escape into the wilderness is cut short, though, when the angel of the Lord finds her at a spring in the wilderness. The angel asks her, "Hagar, slave-woman of [Sarah], where have you come from and where are you going?" (Genesis 16:8). Hagar tells truthfully that she is fleeing from Sarah. The angel of the Lord tells her, shockingly, to return and "be abused by her" (v. 9, where once again that verb *'innah* appears, which often suggests sexual humiliation in the Bible).

This is a terrible moment of Scripture for me, where God (who here appears very masculine) tells an enslaved woman to go back to her enslaver to be abused. I want to reject this statement and everything it stands for. But I wonder if, perhaps, the angel of the Lord was working strategically for Hagar's short- and long-term survival, and for her son's as well. Hagar, pregnant and alone in the wilderness, is unlikely to survive long enough to give birth to Ishmael. If somehow she does, how will she make it through the birth by herself? Perhaps the angel of God is telling Hagar that her path to freedom has to pass through simple survival before she can really make it to flourishing. But flourishing will come, too. The angel of the Lord tells her next, "I will so greatly multiply your offspring that they cannot be counted for multitude" (v. 10). The blessing of countless offspring—parallel to what God has promised Abraham, is to be Hagar's as well, but first . . . she just has to make it to the next stage. Perhaps God isn't a God of liberation here, but a God of survival . . . a God of "let's just get you through to the next day." It isn't so simple as "just leaving," as our siblings who have been in relationships of domestic violence can attest.

I may find the "return" message unsatisfactory, if not downright disturbing, but Hagar herself feels seen. The first time Hagar speaks in this story is to respond to the angel of the Lord (who might as well be God himself, so close are the associations between God and his messengers). She tells him first that she is running away, but then she does something really extraordinary: she *names* God. Especially in the ancient world, names are powerful; a name tells the significance of something, and the one who does the naming holds some degree of sway over the thing that is named. (Ever read the fairy tale Rumpelstiltskin?) So when Hagar actually names God, it is an unlikely moment in which this survivor of sexualized violence, a slave woman, wields unexpected power. She names God *El-roi*, because, as she says, "Have I really seen God and remained alive after seeing him?" (v. 13).

El-roi. God who sees. For Hagar, though God has told her to return to an abusive situation, she feels truly seen. Maybe for the first time. When God looks at Hagar, he doesn't see a cog in the wheel of his own wants and needs, as did Sarah. He doesn't see a body that he could use as he wills, as did Abraham. He doesn't see a slave woman who is abusable and disposable. When God looks at Hagar, he knows where she has been, that she has in the past and will again in the future experience *abuse*, and he names it as it is with that now-familiar word, *'innah*. Yet when he looks at her, he also sees a powerful mother of a nation. From her will come life as her son Ishmael is born and begins her line. But first, God knows that Hagar has to walk her tired and pregnant feet back home to a place she can survive. For Hagar, being seen in that way gives her whatever it is that she needs to keep walking the difficult road ahead of her.

Hagar remains with Sarah and Abraham for another fourteen years, until Ishmael is a youth, and *finally*, Sarah gives birth to her own biological son, Isaac. Yet again, though, Sarah's tendencies toward abusive behavior cycle to the surface when she senses some level of competition with Hagar. When she sees the two boys playing together, Sarah comes unglued. She demands to Abraham, "Cast out this slave woman with her son; for the son of this slave woman shall not inherit along with my son Isaac" (Genesis 21:10). To his credit (although it's not enough!), Abraham is distressed about this news. But since God assures Abraham that Ishmael will have a great nation made from him as well (that is, the mother-and-son pair will not die in the wilderness), Abraham sends them away with a few supplies. The two come close to dying of thirst. Hagar wails to heaven and turns away from her son, unwilling to watch him die so unfairly and needlessly in the wilderness. But God responds to the direness of the situation. "Do not be afraid," the angel of God reassures her (v. 17). And once again, the God Who Sees responds with the practical resources to ensure survival. Hagar, who has been seen, now can see for herself: there is a well of water available for her son to drink.

This story powerfully shows how God refuses to abandon people who have been stripped of power, including survivors of sexual violence. God makes himself known to Hagar through presence and conversation, through provision of needs and blessing. At the end of the story, Hagar's wounds from the long time she lived with Abraham and Sarah are probably not fully healed. But I would bet Hagar knows that God has been working on her behalf all along. God restores power to her as a matriarch in a line all her own.

WHEN HEALING HAPPENS AFTER ABUSE

In one of my first semesters as a teaching assistant in my PhD program, I led a class discussion on the story of Hagar, Sarah, and Ishmael. To my surprise, it didn't go so well. Many of the students, reading closely, encountered many of the difficulties with the text that I have pointed out here. Other students did not see Hagar as a survivor of abuse. They suggested that the students who pointed out these features of the text were "reading into" the story, projecting their own experiences in ways that erased the original meaning and purpose of the text. Another student, a man I'll call Jay, made an even bolder claim. To paraphrase him, he said something like, "Sure, I can see how Hagar was abused. But she had to go through that to get the divine blessing! Her abuse ultimately made her blessed."

There was a brief moment of shocked silence in the room, and then the room erupted. Most of my female students were in a hurry to tell Jay exactly how messed up they thought his theology was. Most of my male students seemed keen to melt into the floor, avoid any association by gender with Jay, or both. Voices started piling over one another, and no one was really being heard.

I struggled internally in that moment. I didn't know whether I wanted to rescue Jay from the women who were so convincingly and passionately articulating their own distaste for his position or let them continue to rip him to shreds. Ultimately, I did step in to slow the flow of conversation and let Jay have a chance to speak up for himself a bit more.

In all fairness to Jay, what he articulated is no different from the interpretive moves that are made, at least implicitly, by many churches. The idea is that, somehow, the redemption that arrives at the end of these experiences of sexualized abuse is sufficient to mitigate the pain of the abuse itself. To use Jay's term, the "blessing" removes the bite. God was using our abuse for a greater purpose . . . and even, perhaps, for our own good. Romans 8:28 would seem to be a helpful proof text for this theology: "All things work together for good for those who love God."

Few things are more painful to hear than the assertion that God's blessing is contingent on sexualized violence, that our redemption, in fact, requires us to experience this type of pain. I also want to propose that nothing could be further from the truth of God's goodness. I do believe that God is striving for a good end for each of us . . . and, to return to Romans 8, I believe that nothing, even sexualized violence, can keep us from God's love. But the love of God has to contend with real—some would say satanic—evil. I believe that this evil actively resists the good that God has intended for the world. Sometimes, often, this evil lives within the hearts of humans. It originates outside the goodness and love of God. For that reason, I always read Romans 8:28 in step with Genesis 50:20: "You intended it to harm me, but God devised it for good to accomplish what is now being done" (my translation). In other words, God turned the situation around. God creatively devises ways for what is evil to morph instead into something that brings life to us and gives life to others.

God does not intend sexualized violence as a blessing . . . but sometimes, through God's miraculous work in the world, the most terrible experiences that we can imagine propel us down paths that, somehow, lead us back to life.

BATHSHEBA AND DAVID: ROYAL RAPE (2 SAMUEL 11)

Like Hagar, Bathsheba finds herself in no position to resist the powerful advances of a man. David is king of Israel, and Bathsheba is the wife of one of David's soldiers, Uriah. Uriah is not himself an Israelite; his name appears in conjunction with "the Hittite," a strong suggestion that he is an outsider within David's kingdom and has obtained his position as one of David's "mighty men" (2 Sam. 23:39) after years of political machinations and personal struggles (compare with Joseph, Daniel, and Mordecai, each of whom rises in the political ranks of a foreign kingdom, but at no small price). The foreignness of Uriah means that he must tread carefully himself—as the events in the story confirm, one wrong step may cost him his life.

David sees Bathsheba taking a bath on the rooftop in the evening. The story tells us that Bathsheba was very beautiful, but that's about it. There's no mention of whether David loved her at first sight or even wanted her at all: the fact that there was a beautiful woman—a woman who is not *his*—bathing on a rooftop near him was enough to prompt David's next steps. He sends his messenger to Bathsheba. She has been summoned by royal command—what choice does she have but to say yes to whatever he wants?

But David didn't plan well for what would follow. The first words that Bathsheba herself speaks in the story are "I am pregnant." David must know now that his unrighteousness may be discovered; Uriah has been away at war, unavailable to father a child. He needs to find a way to make it appear that Uriah is the father. So he attempts to send Uriah back into his house to wash his "feet," which in biblical times could be a euphemism for his genitals, and bribe him with gifts.[2] With a proverbial wink and a nod, David tries to encourage Uriah to have sex with Bathsheba and thus be able to claim paternity. But Uriah sleeps at the entrance to the palace and refuses to have sex with his wife. Even getting Uriah drunk doesn't do the trick!

David is desperate to save his reputation. He's worried about being perceived not as a rapist (after all, he's the king . . . presumably he can do whatever he wants to whomever he wants) but as an adulterer. His desperation escalates to plotting an assassination. He commands his general, Joab, to plant Uriah in battle where the fighting is heaviest and then abandon him. Uriah the Hittite dies according to plan. The story says that Bathsheba mourns for him, and while this grieving fulfilled cultural expectations, I take the inclusion of this fact as an indication that she truly loved her husband. She did not want to have sex with another man. Bathsheba, raped by David, and now bereaved of her husband, is all alone.

The result of David and Bathsheba's union is a child who dies. The prophet Nathan tells David that as punishment for the liaison, not only will David's house be filled with war forever, but his own child, conceived with Bathsheba, will die. In other words, Bathsheba suffers the loss of her child for what may well have been an unwilling sexualized relationship. David committed adultery and even rape, yet Bathsheba bore the burden of the punishment of losing her child. I myself have not experienced infant loss, but I know from friends who have lost a child that it is one of the most devastating experiences a person can have.

The stakes are always lower the more power a person has. David can rape with relative social impunity because he is a man, and even more than that, he is the king. Whatever fallout there will be from the episode, David could be confident that it would be worse for Bathsheba than for him. David can use his power both to get Bathsheba exactly where he wants her and to do his own damage control, which means that he can sustain his own public relations campaign.

But King David is not exempt from God's scrutiny. God, having observed David's adultery—perhaps even more crucially, his rape of Bathsheba—directs the prophet Nathan to confront him. Nathan tells a parable of a man whose only lamb was cruelly stolen and slain by a rich man. David cannot help but realize that God is seeing him in this story, and he knows that his crimes have been detected. Granted, the imagery of the woman as the lamb, and thus property of the man, reflects an inherently androcentric vision of marriage. Nevertheless, God's interception of David's wrongful efforts to hide his sexualized violence remains a powerful witness. Even David's crimes come to light despite his role as king of Israel.

POWER AND SEXUALIZED VIOLENCE

What's fascinating to me about the Bible is that so often, these ancient stories that present themselves as founding stories of culture itself speak profoundly into the struggles we face today. This is true even of sexualized violence. From the beginning, questions of power and questions of sexualized violence are closely linked. The three women written about in this chapter are each a survivor of sexualized violence, and each of their stories unfolds a little differently, but in the end, power dynamics group them together. Sarah, Hagar, and Bathsheba experience a stripping away of their power as a more powerful individual coerces them into a position where their bodies are disposable.

These stories of power imbalances bring up the tricky concept of consent. It may not even be meaningful to talk about "consent" in the biblical world. When women are not considered autonomous beings and their fortunes are mainly dictated by what's advantageous for the men of the household, women's "consent" to sexual intercourse doesn't hold significant weight. But there are certain times in Scripture (and in our world today) when the notion of consent becomes even more confounded . . . when the stakes of saying no are so high they might even cost someone's life. The stories of Bathsheba and Hagar seem to be two of these. In Hagar's case, she is the slave of wealthy land and livestock moguls. If she refuses their designs for her to become their surrogate, they may decide they have no further use for her and kill her. In Bathsheba's case, she is the wife of an elite soldier in David's army. If she protests, David may retaliate both against Bathsheba and against her husband (which, it turns out, he does anyway; she truly is in a double bind).

What can saying yes really mean when there's an imbalance of power to this degree? When a person has reason to fear repercussions for refusal, I think refusal means very little. What this can develop into for victims of sexualized violence is a real sense of guilt. We might feel that we have betrayed what we stand for when we've had sexualized contact with someone where such a power imbalance exists. Perhaps we might feel that our hurt and anger are invalid emotions, for, after all, we "agreed" to a sexual encounter. In these moments, it's crucial to remember that, as these biblical stories remind us, not everything that looks like consent (or at least seems like the absence of refusal) is truly consent. We're sometimes faced with impossible choices where, tragically, accepting sexualized violence seems like the safest route out of a situation.

Imbalances of power are some of the greatest contributors to situations of sexual violence. But the funny thing about power is that it's always morphing. In some moments of my life, I feel quite powerless. To give a trivial example, when something goes wrong with my car and I take it to the shop, I feel totally powerless. Usually, because I'm female (and also quite possibly because it's obvious I know nothing about cars), I feel at the mercy of my mechanic, who is male. If he tells me

I need a $1,200 car repair because my transmission needs to be replaced, who am I to question him? If he tells me I should probably give up, go home, and buy a new car . . . I don't really have the knowledge to disagree with him. However, in a different context, I know I am quite powerful. As a professor, students often ask me to write them recommendations for graduate school or jobs. Usually, the students have no access to these letters before or after I submit them, so technically, I could write whatever I want. I could say that a student is the most brilliant person I've met, or that the student really has no place in the classroom. While I try to practice good ethics and tell students honestly whether I can write a good recommendation for them before I agree to do so, this is just one of the ways in which my professional position affords me power.

Biblical characters and many of the rest of us are much like this, too; our powerlessness in one situation stands in stark contrast to our power in another situation. Our victimization in one context (like Sarah's imperiled position in Pharaoh's household) doesn't make us immune from making others into *our* victims in another (like Sarah's abuse of Hagar).

But to play with the imagery of "living on the wrong side of the tracks," I think many of us tend to settle more on one side of the tracks than the other . . . not just in terms of where we live (although the neighborhoods where we live can have a lot to do with how much power we have), but in terms of how much power we wield in our day-to-day lives. As a straight white woman with a PhD and a comfortable salary, I hold a lot more power than many other members of the global community. In my current context in the United States, America's violent idolatry of whiteness is increasingly becoming exposed through the crucial advocacy of groups led by Black, Indigenous, and other people of color. Black and Brown people, who have been treated as subhuman in the history of the United States, have pointed out the many ways that white supremacy has permeated every area of our culture.

One of the ways that white supremacy has manifested itself is through sexualized violence. In particular, Black women living in the United States have been denied the fundamental right to bodily autonomy. Enslaved women in the United States often experienced rape at the hands of white masters. They gave birth to children fathered by these men, children who faced an uncertain future, as their white fathers might or might not acknowledge them as their children, and more often than not considered them merely an expansion of their human property. Enslaved women watched their own children starve or be sold away while being coerced into being wet nurses for white children. In the era of Jim Crow laws in America, Black women were raped by white men with impunity, while Black men were caricatured as aggressively hypersexual and a threat to white women. Any invented advances of Black men toward white women could then be used as a reason for white mobs to lynch Black men. This is the story of Emmett Till, a fourteen-year-old Black boy who was lynched after a white woman falsely suggested that he acted flirtatiously toward her. Black men and boys' torture and lynching could also involve sexual humiliation by white people, as Black men and boys were sometimes castrated as part of white mobs' efforts to totally dehumanize the people they targeted.

This is not ancient history. Sexualized violence and racial bigotry in America are still tied together. The #MeToo movement emerged from the reality that sexualized violence takes place across many power imbalances, including race. Unfortunately, many white #MeToo advocates have not been good about acknowledging and combating the awareness that racial injustice and sexualized violence conspire insidiously. Many white women who type #MeToo do so without knowing that this movement was founded by a Black woman, Tarana Burke, in 2006. While Burke has explicitly said that #MeToo was intended for anyone to highlight their own experience of sexual harassment, white women in overwhelming numbers came to dominate the movement and have silenced the voices of Black and Brown women.

The story of Black racial oppression in America and its relationship to sexualized violence, which I've referred to here in broad strokes, is just one of the many we could tell. There are so many more stories to tell—stories of how undocumented women in United States may be reluctant to report sexualized violence (even more so than Americans who are citizens) because they fear deportation, stories of how women fleeing political and religious persecution traded sex (under duress) for safe passage for their families, stories of how vulnerable youth are often tricked and drawn into the sex trade, and stories still untold.

The #MeToo movement has exposed many stories that remind me of Hagar's and Bathsheba's, stories where the details may be blurry, stories where a powerful person (most often a man) abused his position of power to pursue a sexualized encounter. Often, stories like these are decades old. They've emerged in every sector of our society, including politics. In the United States, powerful men on both sides of the political aisle have been credibly accused of sexualized violence. Often, the narrative goes something like this: A young woman was interning, or was a low-level aide, to an ascendant politician decades ago. He made many advances, some of which might have seemed relatively small and others which became too big to ignore. The young intern or aide did not feel she was in any position to say no—perhaps she did not have language to rebuff the unwelcome encounter that she was experiencing. She had her own future to think about, and one swift way to drop down the political ranks was to accuse a powerful man of misconduct. She knew she would be called names. She might lose her job. She might get death threats. So she did not say no. She did not tell her story publicly—at least not in full.

The sad thing is, she was right. Decades later, she would see this powerful man in the headlines, about to become an even more powerful leader in politics. Around her, the #MeToo movement was starting to swirl. She wondered if this might be the moment she needed to act, if perhaps, by some miracle, her story would be better received now than it would have been back then. So she sent some letters, released some statements to the press. The backlash was immediate and overwhelming. She was called names. Her private records were dug up and used to call her crazy. She got death threats in the mail and over the phone. In the end, it was hard to tell exactly who cared about her story: the powerful man continued to rise, while she continued to sink.

But it did matter. It has mattered to survivors, who could begin to see each other in the darkness, like those faces illuminated by candles in the dark Christmas Eve service, who could begin to say to one another, "I believe you, even if no one else does. I will stand beside you, even if no one else will. I will be a witness to your story, in a world that tries to make you ever more invisible."

I note these stories briefly, painful as they are, to show that sexualized violence is something that does not merely flourish on its own, but thrives particularly well when imbalances of power are allowed to stand. Also, the intersection between sexualized violence and all the other kinds of power in our world make it very possible that a person may become a survivor, yet still participate in another person's oppression . . . including taking part in another's experience of sexualized violence.

All of these realities about the systems of oppression that surround us need to shape the ways we read the Bible. No, not all the oppressions of our world today were part of the social context in which the Bible was written. (Some of them, however, such as the weaponizing of bodies and sex in ways counter to God's design for the world, clearly *were* part of biblical times just as they are part of our times.) However, wherever and however we grew up; however we learned to read the Bible; and however we were and are used to hearing it preached are imbedded in it. Nobody reads the Bible neutrally.

GOD AS WITNESS

These experiences in which survivors of sexualized violence have seen power abused matter deeply to God. The God whom Hagar encountered in the wilderness and boldly named El-roi, the God who sees, is the God of the survivors who bravely told their stories—at great cost to themselves—and said #MeToo. In a country where the justice system often fails to be just, where the body one inhabits and the position one holds have so much to do with whether one's testimony is taken seriously, the Bible bears witness to a God who really does see all. For some of us, God's witness to our experiences of sexualized violence matters greatly because no one has heard us or believed us before.

There's a level of inscrutability to the experience, even to the person who experienced the event as a victim. Parts of memories stand out in vivid color, while other parts seem blurry and uncertain. When survivors try to tell about the events, the chains of events they narrate often seem choppy, inconsistent, and confusing, and their stories sometimes change. (A reason, albeit a poor one, that survivors' reports are often doubted.) There are questions about these experiences that often go unanswered—forever. If there's an inscrutability to sexualized violence, it's an inscrutability that's matched only by the depths and mystery of God's own wisdom and love. God sees. God knows. God understands.

The Christian hope is that one day, we will see and know and understand as well. In 1 Corinthians 13:12, Paul writes, "For now we see in a mirror, dimly, but then we will see face to face. Now I know only in part; then I will know fully, even as I have been fully known." One day, perhaps only at the end of all things, but hopefully a lot sooner than that, I believe that the truths of our lives will be fully seen and acknowledged. In the book of Job (in one of the few relatively happy parts in the narrative!), Job says, "I know that my redeemer lives, and after all he will rise upon dust" (19:25, my translation). Here, Job, who has been addressing God in legal courtroom style, trying to prove that he has suffered innocently, has a moment of hope as he contemplates his redeemer (go'el) vindicating his pleas. This image of God as an authoritative witness in a courtroom provides immense reassurance to those of us who have seen our stories disbelieved and mocked. Who could reasonably argue with the witness of God?

For some survivors, seeing how power is abused in our world in ways that allow and even encourage sexualized violence may undercut their confidence in God's *power* as part of their healing. We might even wonder if God can be exempt from the type of corruption that often comes from power. After all, much of the suffering that survivors of sexualized violence experience is done in God's name. For me, though, God's hands are the only place where this type of power feels safe. That's because, for me, the life and passion of Jesus Christ show us what God does with power. Given a position of privilege—*divine* privilege, even—Jesus gives it all away. Jesus' power goes not toward controlling others or exposing their vulnerability, but toward emptying himself to close the gap between heaven and earth. He is our perfect model of how to handle privilege in a godly way.

God holds all authority of the world that belongs rightfully and only to God and uses it to bear witness to the *least* powerful and to find a way for them out of the wilderness and into freedom and healing. This is the God who bears witness to our stories of sexualized violence: the God who takes on power only to give it away for our sake. This is a power that can be trusted.

2

BEARING WITNESS TO OURSELVES AND ONE ANOTHER

Sexualized violence has different witnesses—witnesses who survive the violence itself, witnesses who act as bystanders and do not intervene, witnesses whose loved one passes through this trauma. Just as there are different types of witnesses, so there are different ways of bearing witness to trauma. Our bodies, minds, and spirits—all so intimately interconnected—express the stories of the trauma we've experienced in different ways. For some, narrating and re-narrating the story is the path to healing. For others, silence is the witness of the pain they suffer and contains an implicit no to the violence of the past. For others, the trauma of sexualized violence unfolds through illness, both mental and physical, as our bodies retain the memories of what we have passed through in symptoms that may belie our attempts to normalize our lives. For still others, patterns of relationships persist beyond a single traumatic event and sometimes tell a story of pain that our lips would never share.

In this chapter, I'll talk about survivors of sexualized violence themselves, and how their experiences and reactions
bear witness to pain, but also to resilience and hope. I'll also
talk about those loved ones of survivors, who often experience
trauma through their connections to survivors. For those who
want to be allies for survivors, I'll explore in particular how
biblical texts suggest we can accompany survivors in their
journeys to healing and hope—not taking away their pain,
not rewriting their stories, but instead offering the space and
advocacy that survivors need to continue on their journey.

Significantly, the broadening understanding of trauma
includes not only those who are direct survivors of an event,
but also their loved ones. Sometimes the term *secondary
trauma* is used for those who have not *themselves* experienced
a life-endangering, frightening event but have seen their loved
ones go through it. However, "secondary" trauma downplays
how serious, significant, and life-altering it is for a loved one of
a survivor to experience an event like this. The *Diagnostic and
Statistical Manual of Mental Disorders* (DSM-5) now includes
the experience of having a loved one experience a life-threat-
ening event as one of the diagnostic criteria for PTSD. In other
words, being a loved one to a survivor *is itself* a trauma. As
we'll see in the Bible, the loved ones of survivors are often
deeply affected by the trauma their loved ones have experienced, playing out their own trauma in ways unanticipated
and sometimes devastating.

BEARING WITNESS IN OUR BODIES: DINAH (GENESIS 34)

Two stories about women in the Bible are often read side by
side: those of Dinah, daughter of Jacob, and Tamar, daughter
of David. Both of these stories are read by most people as

accounts of sexualized violence. In Dinah's story, appearing in Genesis 34, the young woman has "gone out" to meet neighboring women when Shechem son of Hamor, the Hivite, grabs her and "defiles/rapes" (the word '*innah*, often used for "rape," is used here) her. Shechem claims to be so drawn to Dinah that he must have her hand in marriage. In the marriage negotiations, Dinah's brothers deceive the Hivites into believing they will allow Shechem to marry Dinah, if only all the Hivite men will be circumcised. But when the Hivite men are still in pain from the circumcision procedure, the brothers sneak into the Hivite camp and massacre all the men and take women, children, and property as their booty.

When I read the story of Dinah, particularly as a person who is attuned to sexualized violence in these stories, one thing more sticks out to me: Where is Dinah's voice? The biblical story in Genesis 34 does not contain a single instance of her speech. We don't know what Dinah is thinking when Shechem initiates sexualized contact. We don't know what Dinah is thinking when Hamor, the father of Shechem, approaches her father, Jacob, to ask for her hand in marriage. We don't know what Dinah is thinking when her brothers enter the city of the Hivites to plunder and commit murder.

This passage is difficult to interpret because there is not a specialized word for "rape" in biblical Hebrew. In many cases in the Bible, when I see the word '*innah*, I translate it as "rape" because the story seems to suggest it so strongly that it's hard to imagine reading it otherwise (at least when intentionally reading the Bible through the lens of survivors). However, the *most* clear instances in the Bible where '*innah* can be translated as rape seem to be where '*innah* appears together with a word that deliberately suggest physical force, like the verb *hazaq*, which is often translated as "grab." That's not what happens

in the story of Dinah. Shechem "takes" Dinah (using the verb
laqaḥ). While this word may sound just as violent and noncon-
sensual as the verb *ḥazaq*, it's really a very routine word used
in the Hebrew Bible to convey the relationship between a man
and a woman as a man "takes" a wife. The next verb in the
sequence of the sentence is *šakab*, "lie with," which is a fairly
neutral word that often refers to sexual intercourse. And then
finally comes *'innah*, by far the most difficult of these words to
translate, and it's tricky to choose the right word—especially
since we do not hear Dinah's voice at all in the story. Getting
a "read" on her body language and affect—essential aspects
of human communication that convey much about a person's
consent or lack thereof—is simply not possible in this story.

It's even been debated whether Genesis 34 is a "rape text"
at all. However, one thing needs to be made clear about this
story: Dinah's silence can also be a witness. Perhaps she does
not speak because she knows it would not do any good. The
more powerful men in this story can override her wishes
whether she expresses them or not. (After all, the effect is the
same anyway in the story of Tamar and her brother Amnon,
which I'll discuss shortly). She may feel that the safest thing
to do is keep her mouth shut. But her silence *does not equal
consent*. It does not equal submission.

I believe that Dinah's silence is a form of witness. For many
people who experience sexualized violence, silence is part of
the experience. The commonly used dichotomy of "fight or
flight" is not the human body's only responses to trauma;
among others, "freezing" can be a way that humans protect
themselves from harm that is being done to them. Our bodies
can sometimes simply shut down when they're in harm's way.
Silence can also come from the fear that making a sound will
trigger even greater violence from an attacker. People who did

unsolicited contact, silent as Shechem seeks her out as his wife, silent as her brothers exact their revenge on Shechem's household and people, Dinah still bears witness to the effects of sexualized violence working themselves out in her body and her mind. Her silence in no way legitimates what she has gone through or signals her submission. It, just like a verbal or other physical type of response, reflects how Dinah needs to function to survive the excruciatingly difficult situation in which she finds herself.

IT'S REALLY NOT ABOUT YOU: DINAH'S BROTHERS AND FATHER

Yet Dinah is not the only person in Genesis 34 who responds to the crisis. Jacob and his sons react as well—although Jacob's reaction seems oddly muted compared to that of his sons: "Now Jacob heard that Shechem had defiled his daughter Dinah; but his sons were with his cattle in the field, so Jacob held his peace until they came" (v. 5). Interestingly, in a story where other characters have big emotions (Shechem's soul "was drawn to Dinah," v. 3; the brothers go on to commit murder in their rage), Jacob's emotions are subdued. Perhaps he is resigned as a function of age and experience; he has already seen how destructive anger can be upon a family (recall his own flight and estrangement from Esau years earlier). Or perhaps he believes he can avoid experiencing emotions of his own because his sons will soon be there to do all the feeling that anyone could possibly muster. Regardless, Jacob will soon experience the fallout of his unaddressed family dysfunction; he *will* have to face the embedded pain in his family dynamics sooner or later (and it turns out that Joseph's slavery in Egypt and Benjamin's peril will mean all of this happens on the sooner side of things).

The entrance of the sons onto the scene coincides with the arrival of Hamor, the father of Shechem: "And Hamor the father of Shechem went out to Jacob to speak with him, just as the sons of Jacob came in from the field. When they heard of it, the men were indignant and very angry, because he had committed an outrage in Israel by lying with Jacob's daughter, for such a thing ought not to be done" (vv. 6-7). It's unclear what the "problem" is here from the perspective of Dinah's brothers. The word *rape* is never mentioned. The word translated here as "outrage" is the Hebrew *nebala*. Perhaps more literally it simply means a foolish thing, a mistake. The mistake here is not the possibility that Shechem forced Dinah into a sexualized act, but that the act itself crossed boundaries that should not be traversed. Namely, a man should not, in the eyes of this cultural setting, have sex with a virgin, especially not without her father's consent. But even more pressingly, people should not have sex outside the bounds of their own cultural group (exogamy).

This problem of exogamy comes up as Hamor proposes a deal to Jacob that goes far beyond Dinah herself. Hamor is trying to right the problem that Shechem raised of sex outside of one's cultural group by, in effect, merging Jacob's people with the Hivites. The deal he proposes goes like this: "The heart of my son Shechem longs for your daughter; please give her to him in marriage. Make marriages with us; give your daughters to us, and take our daughters for yourselves. You shall live with us, and the land shall be open to you; live and trade in it, and get property in it" (vv. 8-10). Crucial elements of becoming one people—two-way marriage agreements and shared space in which to live and flourish—will bind together the Hivites and Hebrews.

Shechem seems to surmise (rightly!) that he's going to have to throw even more into the bargain to pacify Jacob's incensed sons. So the next part of their entreaty is directed explicitly to the brothers as well as their father: "Shechem also said to her father and to her brothers, 'Let me also find favor with you, and whatever you say to me I will give. Put the marriage present and gift as high as you like, and I will give whatever you ask me; only give me the girl to be my wife'" (vv. 10-12). Little do they know that Dinah's brothers will propose physical alteration of their bodies to match those of the Israelites through circumcision. And yet the Hivites are willing to comply.

A subtle yet crucial point is that Dinah seems to be dwelling among the Hivites this entire time. When posing their demand to the Hivites, the threat is *removal* of Dinah from the Hivites: "But if you will not listen to us and be circumcised, then we will take our daughter and be gone" (v. 17). This point gets emphasized further after Dinah's brothers have committed the murder against the Hivites: "They killed Hamor and his son Shechem with the sword, and took Dinah out of Shechem's house, and went away" (v. 26). The perhaps surprising aspect of this arrangement is that Dinah's father and brothers did not request Dinah's return in the interim before the marriage would take place or even before the engagement was formalized.

That the brothers leave Dinah in the house of Shechem during this time raises questions for me. I wonder what this interim was like for Dinah. Was she glad to escape her home with many brothers and live with her lover? Or was this a terrifying period in which there was no refuge from a man who had never sought her consent for sexual activity and was repeatedly raping her? While Dinah herself would have known these answers, and her bodily experience would have borne witness to her truth, we, as readers, *cannot* know what it would have been like for her.

Yet the brothers (or her father, Jacob, for that matter, but he has receded so far into the background of the story that the brothers assume most of the acting responsibility) do not appear interested in Dinah's experience of the incident, or even if she is all right living with the Hivites. They are concerned with her virginity (and lack thereof) as a reflection on their own honor. Whether the incident with Shechem was a rape makes little difference to them: the point is that Shechem is an outsider, and union with him of any type, including a sexual encounter, besmirches their honor as Israelite men.

It is this sense that the family's honor, particularly the status of the *men*, has been breached that prompts Dinah's brothers to carry out the massacre that comes next. Simeon and Levi wait three days, until the circumcision of all the Hivite men has taken place and they are still in pain, to enter their city stealthily. They kill every male within the city (with special mention in verse 26 that Hamor and Shechem are among those who are killed). The killing of the men then enables Simeon and Levi to carry out the rest of their plan, to loot the livestock and fields of the Hivites. The women and children come last— these are captured and taken back to Jacob's family. It seems safe to assume that the women will be forced to marry or have sexualized contact with Jacob's sons, perpetuating what may well be a theme of rape in the narrative. Dinah also comes home with her brothers, yet the narrative gives no word on her reaction to the carnage that, theoretically at least, was done on her behalf.

This concern for their *own* status as a function of Dinah's sexual activities is what fuels the brothers' last words at the end of the narrative. Their father, Jacob, is not pleased that the brothers have committed murder (mainly because it inconveniences his relationships with the neighbors), yet the brothers are convinced that they have done what is right to prevent their family from being associated with sexual immorality: "Then Jacob said to Simeon and Levi, 'You have brought trouble on me by making me odious to the inhabitants of the land, the Canaanites and the Perizzites; my numbers are few, and if they gather themselves against me and attack me, I shall be destroyed, both I and my household.' But they said, 'Should our sister be treated like a whore?'" (vv. 31-32). Ultimately, the brothers' concern amounts to a determination to preserve the image of their own family, which involves policing the sexuality of each of its members. They do not care about Dinah's witness, whatever it is, to the experience that she has undergone.

BEARING WITNESS THROUGH LAMENT: TAMAR (2 SAMUEL 13)

I now turn to a story that's often read alongside that of Dinah, involving Tamar, a daughter of David. Unlike Dinah's story, Tamar's witness becomes known through her own words that express her resistance to what happens to her. Amnon, son of David, and Tamar's half-brother, desires to have Tamar. It's not so much that he wants *her* (later in the story, his disgust of her shows how much he does not want her at all) as he wants to have control over her body. Amnon, "sick with love" (2 Samuel 13:2), finds an ally in his friend Jonadab to devise a plan to get Tamar exactly where Amnon wants her. Tamar is directed into Amnon's room to make heart-shaped cakes, where Amnon takes the opportunity to demand that she submit to his request for intercourse. "Come, lie with me, my sister," he insists (v. 11).

What happens next is, for me, one of the most extraordinary moments in Scripture. Not only does Tamar refuse his demand for sex, but her bold denial is also held within Scripture.

No, my brother, do not force me; for such a thing is not done in Israel; do not do anything so vile! As for me, where could I carry my shame? And as for you, you would be as one of the scoundrels in Israel. Now therefore, I beg you, speak to the king; for he will not withhold me from you. (vv. 12-13)

Tamar's prophetic no, couched within shrewd reasoning that *should* convince her half-brother to halt his inappropriate advances, is a moment in Scripture that can challenge our perception that women in Scripture are *necessarily* silent and submissive. Tamar becomes an advocate for herself. She refuses to even pretend that Amnon's harassment is wanted or acceptable. She bears witness to the reality that our bodies are sacred and our own, not for the taking.

Yet to Amnon, Tamar's resistance makes no difference: "But he would not listen to her; and being stronger than she was, he forced her and lay with her" (v. 14). His determination to commit rape no matter what Tamar does points to a broader reality that's often missed when our culture discusses sexualized violence: People can refuse, they can set boundaries, they can do all the "right" things and they can *still* experience sexualized violence.

The story also profoundly points out how sexualized violence is fundamentally about neither desire or love, but power. After Amnon has achieved his goal of sexual contact with Tamar, he is done with her. The act of rape annihilates any feeling of "wanting" he might have believed he had for her: "Then Amnon was seized with a very great loathing for her; indeed, his loathing was even greater than the lust he had felt for her" (v. 15). Since Amnon has achieved his prize, Tamar is of no further use to him. She becomes both unwanted and disposable, and Amnon wastes no time in getting rid of her.

As the object of his disgust, Tamar cannot be removed from Amnon's chambers fast enough.

At this moment a turn takes place in the story that may be painful and all too familiar to survivors of sexualized violence. When Amnon tries to kick Tamar out, she clings to him. She wants to stay. She cries, "No, my brother; for this wrong in sending me away is greater than the other that you did to me" (v. 16). Tamar's reaction might be shocking or horrifying. But her reaction after her rape feels relatable to many survivors of sexualized violence, as well. In that moment of total vulnerability after violation, we can desperately seek something to hold on to. Sometimes, tragically, the only person present with us to cling to is our abuser, as sexualized violence often (though not always) occurs, through the desire of the abuser, in complete isolation. That can mean that we cling to our abuser after our assault.

That we may have turned to our abuser in this moment does not need to be a source of shame. But so often, survivors of sexualized violence experience self-hatred for their willingness to be with their abuser in this moment. Here is a moment where the biblical text gives us a chance to extend to ourselves the empathy we would have for another person. Tamar's clinging to Amnon is deeply relatable. Tamar fears the reception she'll get outside the doors of Amnon's chamber when she, a should-have-been-virgin who has been raped, leaves. She has just experienced someone whom she quite possibly loved and trusted, an older brother, turn on her and hurt her. She *needs* someone to be near her, and there is no guarantee that anyone will ever be there for her again. Amnon is there, and in her emotional need, she longs to be with him.

There is no shame in this, only the tragedy that Tamar cannot guarantee that anyone else will be there to care for her.

Tamar's lament resounds after Amnon kicks her out of his chambers. Her devastation cannot be bound up as she weeps for herself, for the cruel treatment she has experienced, and for the curtailing of possibilities for her future: "But Tamar put ashes on her head, and tore the long robe that she was wearing; she put her hand on her head, and went away, crying aloud as she went" (v. 19). Tamar's grief reflects not only the present trauma but also the realization that her status in the world has substantially changed, as she is no longer a marriageable virgin. She recognizes her loss as something worthy of lamenting aloud. She even dares to draw attention to what has happened, voicing her lament loudly in the halls of her palace.

A STRUGGLING ALLY: ABSALOM

Tamar's brother Absalom swiftly and effectively silences her cries. Absalom says, "Has Amnon your brother been with you? Be quiet for now, my sister; he is your brother; do not take this to heart" (2 Samuel 13:20). A couple of aspects about Absalom's comment here are concerning. First, it seems that he had a good inkling of Amnon's predatory behavior before the rape even happened. Absalom might have been able to step in from the sidelines and prevent it from ever happening. Second, Absalom, though he appears to want to act on behalf of his sister, ends up doing a lamentable job of being an effective ally. He tells Tamar to silence herself and, by implication, to not draw attention to what she has experienced. This type of behavior reinforces the shame that Tamar is very likely already experiencing. Furthermore, although it turns out that Absalom has his own plans for retaliation (ultimately attempting to settle the score with Amnon by killing him), Absalom does not consider Tamar's needs or wishes at all. The recovery process that he envisions is driven completely by his own agenda—and likely his own need to correct the infraction to his honor that the dishonoring of his sister caused. There is no sign that Absalom's own agenda helps Tamar at all; perhaps vocal lament is truly what she needs to begin the healing process, and Absalom deprives her of it.

Unwittingly, then, Absalom, who means to be a supportive older brother to Tamar and an ally to her in her vulnerable position, further contributes to her victimization. In the moments after her assault, he removes her agency in doing the one thing that she knows to do and the thing that feels right: lament.

Furthermore, Absalom is unaware of how his close connection to Tamar and her own trauma is shaping his own emotional experience. Absalom may not think of *himself* as being particularly emotionally vulnerable in the wake of Amnon's rape of Tamar. Yet Absalom's inner world is being formed and changed through his close contact with his sister's trauma. As I'll explore further, Absalom's lack of healing from his own trauma related to Tamar's assault will shape his own life and others' lives in ways he surely does not intend.

Tragically, Absalom's own behavior goes on to mirror what he has seen happen to his sister. Absalom has experienced a loved one's trauma, which then becomes his own trauma. His emotional proximity to Tamar and the lack of opportunity to process what his sister's assault has meant to him or how his own experience is being shaped by it means that the trauma affects his life profoundly. Absalom ultimately engages in what psychologists term "traumatic reenactment," which involves (even unintentionally) repeating the circumstances and events around a prior trauma. Trauma reenactment is a behavior that can sometimes supplant a verbal witness statement. What cannot be spoken (and remember Absalom's insistence on silence after the rape!) is then acted out instead.[1] Absalom himself becomes a rapist. Survivors of abuse, or those who love them and experience the trauma of their harm as well, do not typically become abusers in this way. However, Absalom's behavior here reflects the dangers that can arise from lack of self-awareness of trauma.

Similar to how Amnon's associate sets the stage for Amnon's rape of Tamar, Absalom becomes an abuser with the instruction of another. He carries out rape not even with the pretense of having lust for his victims, but instead as a deliberate bid for power. Absalom, who has been furious with his father's inaction to seek justice for his wronged sister Tamar, is now seeking the throne of Israel and going to war with his father, David. He's willing to use any means to communicate to his father his rage . . . even if that means raping his father's concubines in order to demonstrate *how wrong* his father was to let Amnon's deeds go unpunished.

> Then Absalom said to Ahithophel, "Give us your counsel; what shall we do?" Ahithophel said to Absalom, "Go in to your father's concubines, the ones he has left to look after the house; and all Israel will hear that you have made yourself odious to your father, and the hands of all who are with you will be strengthened." So they pitched a tent for Absalom upon the roof; and Absalom went in to his father's concubines in the sight of all Israel. (2 Samuel 16:20-22)

It's tragically, painfully ironic. Absalom, who was the (albeit misguided and mostly unhelpful) ally of Tamar, now carries out analogous violence on his father's concubines. They become nothing more to him than a means of carrying out his campaign of revenge against his father. Though Absalom's anger is understandable, his behavior is inexcusable. He uses sexualized contact with these women without their consent—rape, properly called—as a ploy in his broader effort to dishonor his father. As is so tragically common in the Bible, the sexual status of women, and whether men can claim that women are exclusively *their* sexual territory, figures into the honoring and shaming of men. The wellness of the women themselves goes unconsidered and undiscussed.

Sometimes, it becomes apparent that people who are walking with survivors are *not* comfortable with all emotional reactions to trauma. This, unfortunately, can happen when loved ones and other allies have not fully processed their prior wounds and histories. They're not sufficiently at ease with their own big feelings to be fully present with someone else's—especially in an emotionally intense situation like recovery from sexualized violence. This, I think, is what is at work when Absalom tells Tamar to be silent. He is not ready—*in himself*—to handle the sheer grief of her lament. It's difficult to know what pain in his own past, what shadows of his current self, so frighten him that he cannot sit with Tamar's raw lament. However, the result is that he cannot deal with the way that *Tamar* needs to deal with the situation. His own agenda—which ultimately involves murder of the rapist, Amnon, takes center stage. Absalom convinces himself that centering his own plan is actually in Tamar's best interests—it will be better for her, he manages to maintain to himself, if she can quiet down and leave taking care of business to the men.

But this is not necessarily the case. Tamar never finds full recovery from her trauma. She lives in her brother's house as a "desolate woman" (2 Samuel 13:20). In other words, her trauma becomes her identity. She is bound to this title, to life only within the walls of her brother's household, forever. Meanwhile, Absalom's supposedly cunning plan for restitution

does not necessarily have helpful results for Tamar. His murder of Amnon gets him banished from David's royal seat of
Jerusalem. Ultimately, the conflict escalates into a wholescale
war with his father, David—one that will leave Absalom dead.
Tamar then loses the one person who, purportedly at least, is
her ally.

I believe that Absalom begins this story as a good person.
I don't think he set out down this path on purpose, a path
that would ultimately lead to his committing rape analogous
to that which his sister Tamar experienced. I do not think,
even, that Absalom's efforts to silence Tamar (though in effect
harmful) were malicious. I do not think he intended the killing
of Amnon as a further silencing of her voice. However, all of
these actions, regardless of Absalom's intentions, were harmful. They took Tamar's voice from her and pushed her further
into a position in which she truly had no say in her own life.

Moreover, Absalom was unable to process what the rape
of his beloved sister did *to him*. The ancient world was not
trauma-informed in the way that, thankfully, our contempo-
rarily contexts are gradually becoming. Especially as a man
fulfilling a narrow set of social norms, he was unable to give
himself permission to hurt, to lament, and to sit with the
emotions that these events evoked for him. Presented with a
crisis—a crisis to his sister's safety and honor, no less—Absalom does what so many of us in "helper" roles are inclined
to do and goes into a solution-driven mode. According to
this theory, eliminating the rapist, in this (often unconscious)
perspective, *should* eliminate the difficult emotions that come
with the rape. But, sadly, the trauma remains. Tamar is still a
"desolate" woman—yet she allows herself to mourn. Absalom, on the other hand, does not explore the full dimensions
of his emotional experience in response to the rape.

But the emotional effects on Absalom emerge in other ways, culminating with his rape of his father's concubines. The trauma that Absalom could not allow himself to express, perhaps for fear of appearing "weak" in the face of the threat of his sister's rape, now manifests itself fully as Absalom reenacts the sexualized violence that traumatized him on the women whom David left to keep the house. He not only rapes the women, but also dramatizes the violence: instead of the rape of one woman (Tamar), now it is ten; instead of the violence taking place within a locked chamber, Absalom carries it out on a rooftop so all of Israel can see exactly how much of a "man" he is. Despite his stoic silence on the issue of the rape, in effect it seems that he is determined to demonstrate to his father exactly how much the injustice of the situation has harmed him.

Absalom's story is a sad one for me, even when Tamar is left out of the equation (which she shouldn't be!). His unraveling points to the need for those who ally themselves with survivors, especially those who are emotionally close to survivors, to recognize the trauma that they are legitimately experiencing. To stand with someone who is recovering from an experience of trauma, we must also recognize our yearning for extra gentleness with ourselves. This is important for our own sake as allies, but also for the sake of those we seek to walk alongside. Without deliberately recognizing and attending to our own emotional needs, the way we respond to our loved one's trauma may actually be an unconscious effort to meet our *own* needs, rather than the survivor's.

This, I believe, is the case when Absalom silences Tamar and kills Amnon; he cannot *himself* emotionally tolerate the distress that her lament (that *she* needs) brings him. But planning Amnon's murder gives him the feeling of control which he lacked in his powerlessness to prevent his own sister's rape. Absalom's rape of David's concubines, rather than helping Tamar at all, addresses his need to vent his anger. Sexualized violence becomes a way for him to express his barely contained rage about the power imbalances he experienced that allow David to absolve Amnon of rape without any accountability. Absalom's responses to his trauma—a trauma that is understandable and valid and deserves redress—take over the story by the end. This is a jeopardy that anyone who loves a survivor should be aware of. We can *think* that by pushing our own trauma aside, we are able to focus more wholeheartedly on the person who has lived through an experience of sexualized violence. But the opposite ends up being true. When we as allies and loved ones act from a place of unexamined trauma, we can end up hijacking the entire narrative.

Second Samuel 13 is strikingly honest in this portrayal of the complicated emotional aftermath of sexualized violence. It portrays a woman's verbal response to sexualized violence in a profound and heartbreaking manner. It exposes many people who have not experienced sexualized violence to the deep difficulty that survivors face as they navigate their paths to healing. It challenges those who support survivors to practice more conscious self-care and, through this, enable themselves to listen more deeply to survivors.

PRESENCE AS WITNESS: LAMENTATIONS

When we lived in Tennessee, my children received books every month from Dolly Parton's Imagination Library. (Thank you so much, Dolly!) One of my favorite selections was a short story called *The Rabbit Listened*, by Cori Doerrfeld.[2] In this book, a young boy named Taylor builds a magnificent, enormous block structure . . . only to have it knocked over by a flock of birds flying by. Taylor is understandably very upset. Several animals come along to try to help, including a chicken, snake, elephant, and kangaroo. They all propose solutions to stifle Taylor's big feelings. But Taylor doesn't want to do any of the things his animal friends suggest—and they, dispirited, leave him on his own. This goes on until finally a rabbit comes and sits with Taylor and, as the title implies, simply listens. It's the rabbit's presence, pure and simple, that allows Taylor to move forward and find a way to reimagine and rebuild what has been broken—on his own terms. This simple children's story encompasses what is sometimes so hard for people to grasp about being an ally to survivors: the gift of presence.

We often underestimate how important our presence is. I believe that as allies to survivors, our responsibility, second only to empowering survivors to reach a place of physical and emotional safety if they are not in one already, is to sit with survivors and bear witness to what they are experiencing. The thoughts and emotions they need to voice may not be ones that we, as allies, are comfortable hearing. We may disagree with the reasoning or emotional tenor of what they have to express. I think that Lamentations may model what bearing witness in this way looks like. Lamentations is a greatly under-appreciated book of five poems that was probably written shortly after the Babylonians destroyed the Jerusalem temple. The poems within Lamentations include the voices of many different speakers. Among these are the voices of a narrator, who introduces the book and its context, and Daughter Zion, a woman who represents the entire people of Jerusalem. Like the people of Jerusalem, Daughter Zion experiences terrible tragedy, including the loss of her children and sexualized violence against her own person. The narrator's point of view is not identical to that of Daughter Zion, and there is a point at which his voice withdraws and he makes space for Daughter Zion to speak. If the narrator of Lamentations were the host of a talk show, he'd be an extraordinarily gracious one; he does not interrupt, correct, or fact-check. He just lets her express the pain that she needs to process.

Notably, bearing witness is all Daughter Zion asks for from her listeners—even from God. Although the situation that Daughter Zion is in is truly terrible—she appears to be widowed, her children are dead or kidnapped, and she has been raped—she does not ask God or anyone else who may be listening to "fix" these things. (Perhaps she knows that there is no "fix" for matters of tragedy.) Her sole request is that all bear witness. This request for witness emerges multiple times throughout Lamentations' poetry. In 1:9, recalling the hateful rape that her enemies have carried out against her, Daughter Zion cries, "YHWH, see my rape! For the enemy has grown" (quotations from Lamentations are my own translation).

Passersby are also invited into the role of witness. In Lamentations 1:12, Daughter Zion directly addresses onlookers, the spectators who have beheld her rape or seen her in her aftermath:

Is it nothing to you, all you who pass by?
    Look and see
if there is any pain like my pain . . .

Daughter Zion's outcry comes from the fact that the onlookers are not really "witnesses" in the proper sense of bearing witness; they have been spectators, there for a show. This is not the kind of witness we want to become; there to gain some kind of emotional gratification from the suffering of others.

The demand for YHWH's witness comes again in 1:20, where Daughter Zion calls on YHWH to behold her "distress."

Again in Lamentations 2:20, Daughter Zion demands that the Lord "look and consider" the abuse carried out against innocents. The greatest request Daughter Zion has in the face of all the trauma she has undergone is simply to have a witness that her suffering is real.

God is silent in Lamentations. Unlike most other parts of the Bible, in which God's voice is heard responding to suffering and breaking in to human reality with tenderness and might, God does not respond to Daughter Zion. In Job, one of the other prominent texts of the Old Testament that deals with the problem of human suffering, Job, the protesting and pious sufferer, receives an answer and is able to respond to God. Why doesn't Daughter Zion get an answer too?

Apparently, the biblical writers thought along the same lines. In a slightly later period, other biblical writers would come along and deliberately craft parts of the book of Isaiah (specifically chapters 40–55 and 56–66, what scholars refer to as Deutero-Isaiah and Trito-Isaiah) as a response to the unresolved issues of Lamentations. In passages of these portions of Isaiah, God speaks and responds to Daughter Zion's complaints, and these responses are connected to Lamentations through a network of literary allusions.

However, that sort of response simply doesn't appear in Lamentations. The author doesn't seem to have a problem with God's silence. But for many readers across the millennia that Lamentations has been in use as a sacred text, divine reticence was a problem. It was for me, as well. *Come on, God . . . can't you just say something already?* Now, though, I'm not so sure it's an issue for me. The response from God comes not through verbal response, but through a silent and enfolding witness to pain and suffering. God takes and holds the pain of Daughter Zion when she blames God, when she blames herself, yet God does not feel the need to jump in with the "correct" answers, whatever they may be. God bears witness to the suffering of Daughter Zion, and is . . . there. Simply there. Wordlessly there.

So also can we, as witnesses, bear witness to the experiences of survivors. We can attend to the pain that is expressed and allow it to mold us and affect us and effect change around us. As we do this, we'll probably find that people who are suffering express emotions that are uncomfortable to us from a theological or moral perspective. It's common for survivors to express hatred of self or others or the systems that have harmed them. As Christians, our theological convictions probably lead us to challenge (at least in our own minds and hearts) many of the things we may hear. Yet we do not need to cast judgment on the thoughts and feelings of survivors . . . even if we may hope and pray they may move into a direction that we believe may be more lifegiving. The beginning is simply a ministry of presence.

BEARING WITNESS WITH BALANCE: OUR ROLE

As Christians, balancing our own needs with caring for someone else's is tricky. After all, if we're all the body of Christ, when one part of the body suffers, we *all* suffer. This is the message—but perhaps also the jeopardy—that Galatians 6:2 describes: "Bear one another's burdens, and in this way you will fulfill the law of Christ." This beautiful verse is perhaps also one of the most complex to unpack when it comes to standing with survivors. The difficult balance to achieve is to make a burden less heavy for another person without then placing a burden on ourselves that is too crushing.

We need to be aware of what burdens we are *truly* able to take on while still maintaining our own health and sanity.

There are some burdens that we simply cannot take on at certain points in our lives, or with certain traumas of our own that we are carrying. Recognizing when a burden is one that we cannot share at a particular point is truly all right, and is honestly a gift to someone who may be struggling. I once spoke with a pastor whose parishioner came to her with a pressing concern of personal trauma that intersected with his own past of having committed an act of sexualized violence. The pastor recognized that, as valid as her parishioner's search for healing and hope truly was, she could not help him carry that burden at that point in her life because of her own status as a survivor. She saw, wisely, that at that moment, she was not the proper companion to continue with this man on his journey of healing, hope, and accountability.

The biblical stories we've explored expose the dangers of not realizing what burdens we are emotionally, spiritually, intellectually, and physically prepared to assume. Even well-meaning witnesses who want to stand alongside survivors as allies often have much to learn. Absalom is not ready to bear the burden of Tamar's trauma all by himself—and, in fact, what Absalom does exposes how harmful it can be to try to *take away* others' burdens instead of carrying them *alongside* survivors. The difficult truth is, as much as we as allies want to take these burdens away, we can't. Despite the experiences of trauma that we carry as loved ones of survivors, aspects of the experience of sexualized violence are simply inaccessible to anyone other than the person who has journeyed through it. The burdens still belong, properly speaking, to the survivor.

In personal relationships (for example, those friendships, familial relationships, and partnerships that exist outside the boundaries of a professional relationship such as with clergy or a therapist), it's also important to remember that there needs to be a level of mutuality. This is the wisdom of Galatians 6:2 when it instructs us to "bear one *another's* burdens." Relationships can't survive very long (at least not in a healthy way) if the outpouring of support is one-sided. In contradiction to Cain's original sin of murder in Genesis 4:9, in which he ironically asks, "Am I my brother's keeper?," we *do* bear responsibility for one another—yet we are more properly *each other's* keeper. There are times in relationships in which one person does "more" than the other to keep the relationship functional, times when one person performs more of a supportive role than the other. But these periods should not last forever. As allies to survivors, we need to ensure that we are not standing in the way of true healing and wholeness by being an entire support system unto ourselves. We need to see our role as empowering survivors to seek out experts in the field of trauma who have the skill set to accompany them through their trauma.

It's impossible to stand with survivors of sexualized violence without *really* listening to them. It should go without saying (but unfortunately, much of the time it has to be said anyway) that survivors deserve to have agency over how they proceed after their trauma. They should have space to react in whatever ways they need to—space to mourn, space to rage, space to be silent, space to talk. Perhaps this reality is best reflected in the idea of balance and a "time for everything" in this beloved passage from Ecclesiastes 3:

> For everything there is a season, and a time for every
> matter under heaven:
> a time to be born, and a time to die;
> a time to plant, and a time to pluck up what is planted;
> a time to kill, and a time to heal;
> a time to break down, and a time to build up;

a time to weep, and a time to laugh;
a time to mourn, and a time to dance;
a time to throw away stones, and a time to gather
stones together;
a time to embrace, and a time to refrain
from embracing;
a time to seek, and a time to lose;
a time to keep, and a time to throw away;
a time to tear, and a time to sew;
a time to keep silence, and a time to speak;
a time to love, and a time to hate;
a time for war, and a time for peace. (vv. 1-8)

The Ecclesiastes preacher offers the wisdom that in God's timing, there's room for all of these complicated (and contradictory) parts of being human. This is especially true of intense, complicated situations arising from sexualized violence. All the emotions, actions, and states that the preacher names are "beautiful in [God's] time " (v. 11 ESV). The reality of the value and necessity of each of these polarities stands against the way that survivors are frequently encouraged to behave in ways that are socially "acceptable."

Romans 12 offers another insight that can encourage allies of survivors of sexualized violence to let the survivors themselves set the course of the healing process. Those who want to be allies to survivors can heed the call of Romans to "rejoice with those who rejoice, weep with those who weep" (Romans 12:15). There can be moments of joy, victory, and progress along the way of the often dark and painful journey of trauma recovery. There can be times of grief, loss, and anger as well. Those who want to be allies of survivors need to be comfortable with the full range of emotion that comes along the journey.

Bearing witness comes in different forms, and it's a powerful role that's taken on by both survivors and allies. We need to be aware of how diverse and complicated the forms of bearing witness actually are, and how our own process of witness-bearing is not necessarily identical to someone else's. When we bear witness, we offer the world a tremendous gift to understand reality in new ways. We give others the opportunity to act toward the ends of justice and peace in line with God's kingdom. Yet along the way, we must be deeply aware of our own needs in the process. By taking responsibility for these needs, we can truly come alongside one another in the healing work we *all* have to do.

3

MEN, TOO

Sexualized Violence Affects Everybody

For several reasons, I wish it didn't need to be said, but it still bears repeating: Men are also survivors of sexualized violence. People of *all* genders can be victims of sexualized violence, but in this chapter, I want to focus specifically on men, because frequently in North America, men's challenges can be very unique as they confront this issue.

There's heightened and unnecessary silence and shame surrounding men's experiences of sexualized violence.

For many people, clergy sexual abuse scandals in the Roman Catholic Church raised a new awareness of the problem of sexual abuse of men and boys. However, this problem goes far beyond the media spotlight on these particular scandals. While a higher percentage of victims of sexualized violence are women, and a minority of these crimes are actually reported, even fewer cases of sexualized violence against men and boys are reported. The Centers for Disease Control reports that one in ten males in the United States have experienced "sexual violence, physical violence, and/or stalking by an intimate partner during their lifetime and reported some form of IPV [intimate partner violence]-related contact" in their lifetime. However, the word *reported* there is crucial: an estimated one in four men have actually *experienced* sexual violence or other forms of abuse by an intimate partner.[1] In other words, there's a major gap between what's being *reported* and what's actually happening to men . . . an even greater gap than between experience and reporting for women.

A huge number of men are carrying the burden of sexualized violence alone. As difficult as sexualized violence is for women to experience and process, there are many well-publicized spaces where women can find healing and hope and many resources developed specifically to address women's sexual trauma. Tragically, the same is much less true for men. I hope that this book can contribute to that ongoing and still unfilled need through pointing out how the Bible speaks into the often silent suffering of men who have experienced sexualized violence.

Fortunately, the Bible is *not* silent on men's abuse, and in this chapter, I want to highlight how Scripture bears witness to men's suffering. It isn't that the forms and patterns of sexualized violence that men face are totally different from those that women face: the issues that other chapters discuss are all still in play. But the way that men experience sexualized violence and its aftermath *is* shaped by how our culture constructs what it means to be a man.

BIBLICAL MASCULINITY: EXPANDING OUR UNDERSTANDING

From where I stand, I have much love and appreciation for Christian cultures in the United States. I say cultures, plural, because there are many different groups of Christians in the United States, and what Christianity means and how it manifests in social behavior can be radically different from group to group. I've been formed by several different communities that have shown me that Christianity is not a monolith, even in the so-called Bible Belt of the southern United States where I am from. I've been part of (and loved) progressive congregations of multiple mainline denominations, a charismatic multiracial church, an evangelical, nondenominational church, and last but not least a Mennonite congregation. All of these congregations have loved me, taught me, prayed for me, and helped form me (in positive ways) into the person I am today.

But I also recognize that elements of the religious communities that raised me have been harmful in many ways to people I love, particularly male survivors of sexualized violence. I have seen this play out in several ways. First, there's the message that sexualized violence is an issue that concerns women. Male survivors can be so accustomed to hearing sexualized violence spoken about with only *women* named as survivors that they may not realize that their experiences may also fall into this category. Then, since only women's suffering is acknowledged, male survivors can feel that whatever pain they *do* feel is illegitimate.

Second, and more broadly, many church communities, wittingly or unwittingly, construct masculinity in a very limited way. In this understanding of masculinity, the "perfect" male is the stereotypical image of the captain of the varsity football team: huge, invulnerable, and stoic. It's definitely true that some men out there fit this persona fairly well, and if you or someone you love is like that, then truly, more power to you. The perfect man, in this construct, defends himself and his family from all types of dishonor. I don't think this idea is inherently bad or objectionable; for many men, the idea of serving one's family by protecting them from outside incursion brings meaning and purpose. The problem, though, is when we become set on having a *single* idea of masculinity as the defining one. There needs to be space for men to decide for themselves what their masculinity will look like—whether it's artistic, logistical, Type B, fashionable, athletic, spiritual, peaceful, queer, and so on, including any combination of the above.

When masculinity is defined so narrowly, as I think it often is both in our culture and in the ancient world of the Bible, one sees how shame can easily arise, especially in scenarios of sexualized violence. If your entire masculinity is wrapped up in being invulnerable and protecting others, what happens if something violates your own bodily integrity? What happens if you become unable to protect yourself from violent onslaught?

The narrow, exclusive definition of masculinity means that an experience of sexualized violence can easily shake a man's understanding of his own masculinity. Men and boys may, for this reason, be even less likely than women and girls to choose to tell their accounts of survival to others. Because of the limited way that we tend to understand masculinity, they have valid reason to fear that they will be seen as less than masculine if they reveal their identities as survivors of sexualized violence. Potential abusers can use this awareness to their benefit. They can manipulate their victims into refusal to disclose the abuse even to those who could and would help them. And they can use fear of sexualized violence as a tool for creating compliance.

All of this means that a huge part of preventing sexualized violence against men, as well as working toward survivors' healing, is broadening the narrow definition of masculinity that feeds this environment of shame. As much as women's movements have done a great job telling women, "It's okay to be bold, it's okay to be athletic, it's okay to be ambitious," men also need to hear, "It's okay to be emotional, it's okay to be vulnerable, it's okay to be artistically expressive." We all need to feel free to live out the spirit and the calling that God has placed in us.

The Bible is one of the places where we can discover a masculinity that isn't solely defined by stoicism and invulnerability. Some of the most moving scenes in Scripture concern the relationship between the friends David and Jonathan. Some interpreters have gone so far as to say the two were lovers. Maybe they were, maybe they weren't, but to me, the point is mainly that men are empowered, even in Scripture, to have emotionally intimate relationships with one another. The two become close while Jonathan's father, Saul, is still king. Originally a favorite of Saul, David quickly loses favor with the king when it becomes clear that David is the new champion of the people. Jonathan engineers a plan to determine whether Saul is really a danger to David. When he figures out that his friend is in danger, the two weep together and swear their loyalty to each other "as the LORD lives."

David doesn't see Jonathan again. Jonathan and Saul are killed in battle. David is crushed, and then delivers an emotional lament over both Jonathan and Saul (his supposed adversary!). Part of it goes like this:

> Jonathan lies slain upon your high places.
>   I am distressed for you, my brother Jonathan;
> greatly beloved were you to me;
>   your love to me was wonderful,
>   passing the love of women.
> (2 Samuel 1:25-26)

David, the man "after God's own heart," is deeply emotional and vulnerable, even where his male friends are concerned.

And he is not alone in Scripture in diverging from what many of us have been told is "biblical masculinity." There's Jeremiah, the weeping prophet. Joseph, who wears a flamboyant coat and weeps when he reconciles with his brothers. There's Jacob, who limps away from a fight. There's Zacchaeus, who is invisible in his society because of his short stature but whom Jesus honors by visiting his house. And more. Whenever we try to say definitively, "biblical masculinity is *this*," the gifted storytellers of Scripture take pains to prove us wrong. Rereading Bible passages like these is, to me, the beginning of recapturing the broadness of what masculinity can be.

There's also a faulty assumption among many Christians that it's inherent in God's plan for men to be the sexual pursuers, courting women and initiating all romantic advancement in the relationship. This is not based in Scripture. The Song of Solomon (or Songs), the long love poem in Scripture that deals explicitly with an erotic relationship between a man and a woman, shows how a woman is actually willing and able to pursue a man. She goes out looking *for him* in the poem, as his absence is too much for her to bear:

> Upon my bed at night
>   I sought him whom my soul loves;
> I sought him, but found him not;
>   I called him, but he gave no answer.
> "I will rise now and go about the city,
>   in the streets and in the squares;
> I will seek him whom my soul loves."
>   I sought him, but found him not.
> The sentinels found me,
>   as they went about in the city.

"Have you seen him whom my soul loves?"
Scarcely had I passed them,
　　when I found him whom my soul loves.
I held him, and would not let him go
　　until I brought him into my mother's house,
　　and into the chamber of her that conceived me.
(Song of Solomon 3:1-4)

Here, it is the woman who goes out and pursues the male love. Although the woman does encounter opposition from the sentinels, both here and elsewhere in the Song, her freedom to pursue her lover is a positive. Nor does the male lover receive any censure for his more receptive role in the relationship at this point. The male and female lovers together offer and receive the affection that makes for a healthy relationship. This mutuality of their relationship is reflected in the lovely refrain spoken by the female love several times in the poem, "I am my beloved's and my beloved is mine" (Song of Solomon 2:16; 6:3).

All that to say, "biblical masculinity" isn't as simple as many people conceive it to be. Manliness can mean physical strength, emotionality, romantic receptiveness, romantic pursuit, aggression, and also tenderness. While the social roles of the biblical world usually granted men more explicit power than women, men in Scripture, as well as women, end up carrying out their lives in ways that belie rigid stereotypes. Working toward a concept of "biblical masculinity" that really speaks to the broadness of experience reflected in Scripture is something that, among other things, is truly critical to address men's experiences of sexualized violence. Men's legitimate fear that having experienced sexualized violence will cause people to diminish their masculinity fosters an atmosphere where men cannot seek out healing and share solidarity in the same way that women are able to. I believe our calling as Christians is to create environments where the fullness of people's createdness in the image of God can thrive. When men feel they must hide parts of their journeys or experience, including sexualized violence, in order to gain acceptance as men, we fail to honor that image of God in them.

This is a good time to remind ourselves that Scripture itself is not internally consistent. In other words, there are many places that include prominent and rigid assumptions about what masculinity and femininity are. There are also places where those definitions appear to be stretched, changed, or discarded altogether. But for the rest of this chapter, I'll look specifically at moments of Scripture where sexualized violence against men appears. These examples point to the ways in which sexualized violence against men thrives both on gender hierarchy (men versus women) and on male shame (the idea that men who don't fit the mold are less than others).

"WITH THE LYING OF A WOMAN": LEVITICUS

Most Christians tend not to pay a ton of attention to Leviticus. Truth be told, even though I'm a biblical scholar, it's not my favorite book of the Bible either. But strangely enough, it's just a couple of verses from Leviticus that tend to have people up in arms. Here they are:

> Leviticus 18:22: "You shall not lie with a male with the lying of a woman; it is an abomination."

> Leviticus 20:13: "If a man lies with a male with the lying of a woman, both of them have committed an abomination; they shall be put to death; their blood is upon them." (These are my own translations.)

I've heard a lot of talk about these verses in conjunction with contemporary conversations about the LGBTQ community. Honestly, I don't think these passages have much to do with the queer people I know and love. It would be hard for the writers of Leviticus to anticipate what same-sex relationships and marriage would look like today—as hard, in fact, as it would be for them to anticipate how male-female relationships would evolve. I think that the church has already spent a lot of time in a vain attempt to debate what really is not debatable: the divinely given worth of LGBTQ siblings in Christ that is not within human power to give or take away. For that reason, I'm not going to spend much time engaging the scripturally based argument against LGBTQ inclusion. I'm more interested in talking about Leviticus in terms of something that is discussed much less: its challenge to sexual violence against men.

Both of these verses, I believe, are reactions to a cultural setting in which sexualized violence against men was normalized as a tactic in war and as a means of social control. Then, like now, men penetrated other men not necessarily because they were gay, but because in certain settings, it was an effective way to show domination. As has been the case with every example of sexualized violence I've brought up throughout this book, it's easy to find examples that link contemporary sexualized violence with the past. A great fear that people anticipating incarceration harbor is that they will be raped in prison. In men's prisons today, men who would otherwise consider themselves to be straight inflict sexualized violence on other men in order to establish themselves as more powerful than others within the prison hierarchy. As terrible as it must be (here, I'm talking about a reality far beyond my own life experience), the perpetrators may do this out of fear for their own well-being.

If they aren't the ones instilling fear in others, they themselves might be the one harmed. While sexualized violence is never excusable, and while I fully believe in justice for its survivors, I think it's important to pay attention to the systems of oppression that form people into those able to commit abuse.

For a moment, I want to turn to the "abomination" that the Levitical writers say will result from two men having sexualized contact. The word here in Hebrew is *to'evah*. From the translation of *to'evah* as "ritual abomination," it would be easy to suppose that when the writers use this word, it refers to a moral evil. However, all kinds of things in the Old Testament are referred to as *to'evah*, and many of them are pretty routine acts. The problem is that they fall outside *Israel's* allotted boundaries based on the law, not that they represent objective moral evil (for example, eating shellfish). The Levitical lawgivers believed that things were best left in the categories to which they belonged. The problem that the Levitical writer is trying to address in Leviticus 18:22 and 20:13 is that people from one category (men) are being treated like they're in another category (women). Essentially, the sexualized violence that the writer is addressing here is problematic because it emasculates men.

This definitely shouldn't be the reason (or at very least the *only* reason) why sexualized violence is a problem. First and foremost, sexualized violence is a problem because it harms people, men, women, and children alike, at their core. Regardless of how we understand our identities, sexualized violence exploits the vulnerability of our bodies, denies our agency, and desecrates acts that, at their best, are life-giving and empowering. Unfortunately, in Leviticus, the only way the text begins to point to the problem of sexualized violence against men is by relying on a strict set of gender roles.

It's explicitly stated in Lev. 18:22 that, in this context, men and women are to have two very different roles when it comes to sexual relationships. In Lev. 18:22 the instruction given is, literally, not to lie with a man with the "lying of a woman." That very statement indicates that the writers had in mind a very particular stereotype of who women were and what women were supposed to do. Women were the ones who "got laid," who were passively penetrated by men. Men, on the other hand, were supposed to be doing the penetrating. Women were supposed to be passive, men were supposed to be active. Women were not endowed with agency (sexual or otherwise); men were their own agents. For a man to cross the boundary from being an active, dynamic, sexual agent to being the one laid with "in the lying of woman" was a *to'evah*, an unacceptable transgression. Because if a woman has so little power, who, after all, wants to be a woman? Not a man, the Levitical writers tell us.

The problem of male rape within the contemporary prison system might help us understand these verses from Leviticus. In the first one, Leviticus 18:22, the Levitical code calls upon the reader to abstain from lying with a man . . . *as with a woman*. This part of the verse indicates the root of the problem being addressed. Men are penetrating men not for sexual pleasure, but to reduce them to the status of women. Now, obviously this verse is problematic. Women are on the bottom of the social pyramid, and for a man to be reduced to the status of a woman is the worst-case scenario.

The second verse of these two, Leviticus 20:13, presents a bigger problem than the first. If Leviticus 18:22 speaks out against male intercourse to prevent rape as a means of shaming men, as I've suggested, then why in the world does 20:13 say that *both* men who are involved in the episode should be put to death? That's kind of the ultimate victim-blaming, isn't it?

Yes. And, unfortunately, that kind of attitude isn't out of place in the ancient world of the biblical texts or in ours. Death in cases of rape isn't foreign to the Bible. Consider Deuteronomy 22:23-24:

> If there is a young woman, a virgin already engaged to be married, and a man meets her in the town and lies with her, you shall bring both of them to the gate of that town and stone them to death, the young woman because she did not cry for help in the town and the man because he violated his neighbor's wife. So you shall purge the evil from your midst.

The assumption is that in a town, where people are supposedly all around, a young woman who is under attack could have gotten assistance by crying out. This, in the deeply wrong worldview expressed here, would mean that the woman who did not cry out actually wanted the encounter. There are so many things wrong with that assumption that it's hard to keep track. First of all, what if the man threatened to kill the woman if she cried out? What if the threat of violence was implied? What if the man had gagged the woman? What if previous trauma caused her to keep silent? What if . . . ?

On the flawed assumption that the rape *could* have been prevented but the woman chose to let it proceed, it's not really treated like rape at all, but instead is handled like a case of adultery. Just before this passage concerning rape, Deuteronomy 22:22 tells how adultery should be dealt with:

> If a man is caught lying with the wife of another man, both of them shall die, the man who lay with the woman as well as the woman. So you shall purge the evil from Israel.

There's no question why Deuteronomy 22:23 follows directly on the heels of this passage. When rape is assumed to be preventable, it isn't treated like rape at all, but instead as adults caught in the act of adultery, since the woman in this case is an engaged woman. The raped woman is then punished accordingly.

All this to say that, tragically, death for survivors of sexualized violence isn't at all out of the range of possibility. So in Leviticus 20:13, it shouldn't come as a huge surprise that men face a double threat: of sexualized violence and of death. Here, I want to draw a direct line of comparison between the "preventable" rape of the engaged woman and the suggested rape of the man. In the case of the woman, the rape is preventable because she "could have" called out for help. In Leviticus 20:13, the reason for the double execution after (what I read as) a potential rape isn't given . . . but I think it's implicit. The man's rape is preventable because he is (supposed to be) a man. According to the way of thinking that Leviticus expresses, a "real man" would not have become vulnerable to another man through military defeat or slavery or other loss of social standing. A "real man" would have been able to fight off his attacker.

In this way of thinking, a man isn't a man anymore if he has been penetrated by a man; he has become "like a woman." Women, in this worldview, can be the equivalent of property. They are in no way the equal of men. To become "like a woman" through penetration is therefore a great insult, and thus an abomination.

SODOM AND GOMORRAH: ATTEMPTED MALE RAPE (GENESIS 19)

Much like Leviticus 18:22 and 20:13, Genesis 19 is a story that has been weaponized against LGBTQ people. For me, the use of this story to condemn "homosexuality" represents a profound abuse of the text as well as spiritual abuse of listeners who are told, through this story, that their lives are insignificant to God. However, it does speak to Scripture's concern with sexualized violence against men. It's this act of attempted sexualized violence, actually, that pushes God over the edge to destroy the cities of Sodom and Gomorrah, as he warned Abraham that he would do.

Today, many people who read Genesis 19–20 and *don't* use it to condemn "homosexuality" think that it instead has to do with hospitality. Where Sodom and Gomorrah are referenced elsewhere in Scripture, same-sex intercourse is never directly the subject of the criticism. There's good scriptural backing for this: Ezekiel 16:49-50 says that the sin of Sodom is its greed in failing to share goods with those who are needy. But I think this assessment of the sin of Sodom doesn't go far enough. The particular absence of hospitality, or maybe better, the presence of strong xenophobia, led to a willingness to humiliate strange male visitors through rape. There *are* problematic sexualized actions in this passage . . . but it's not about sexual orientation, it's about male-on-male rape.

In Genesis 18, God has already made up his mind to destroy the people of Sodom and Gomorrah, and he communicates this plan to Abraham, who strikes up a bargaining conversation with him. It's because of Abraham's mission to establish justice and righteousness in his family tree and for all people that God even bothers to share his intentions with Abraham. God says in verse 19: "No, for I have chosen him, that he may charge his children and his household after him to keep the way of the LORD by doing righteousness and justice; so that the LORD may bring about for Abraham what he has promised him." After that, Abraham, who is quite alarmed by

God's pronouncement of destruction, repeatedly asks God if he will be willing to spare the cities for a certain number of people, down from fifty to ten. Each time, God's response is plain: even for a tiny number of righteous individuals, God is willing to spare the city.

Lot, who is living in Sodom as an outsider, models the hospitality that God's angels, sent from Abraham's dwelling to the city, should be able to expect anywhere. Lot honors them by bowing to them and "press[es] them" (Genesis 19:3 ESV; a clever word choice that foreshadows the sexual pressing of the men that is to come) to spend the night in his own house. (The angel-men would rather spend the night in the square, but Lot is convinced that would be too dangerous; he seems to know already how the powerful in the city of Sodom treat outsiders.) It's at bedtime (another clue that what is about to transpire is of a sexualized nature) when the men of Sodom come calling. They surround the house to increase the prickling feeling that this is a matter of life and death. The men aren't interested in sex for physical satisfaction; they want to penetrate in order to inflict pain and prove their dominance. They call out to Lot, "Where are the men who came to you tonight? Bring them out to us, so that we may know them" (v. 5).

I've heard it suggested that the "knowing" here is just knowing in the more conventional, modern sense, as in "getting to know." But I think there's more at play here. There would be no reason for the men to surround the house, in a way that seems to prevent escape, if the Sodomites were just visiting for a casual conversation. The other cues in the text, like the "pressing" that Lot does to persuade the men and the setting of the story at night, further suggest that something sinisterly sexualized is happening. That's certainly the way Lot understands the story: Lot responds with an attempted diversion of the men by offering his own daughters. He says to the men, "I beg you, my brothers, do not act so wickedly. Look, I have two daughters who have not known a man; let me bring them out to you, and do to them as you please; only do nothing to these men, for they have come under the shelter of my roof" (vv. 7-8).

Lot's first words to the men remind me of Tamar's pleas to Amnon to reconsider his actions. And both Tamar and Lot mount a plea to the aggressors based on commonly accepted moral codes: for Tamar, it is that her rapist Amnon is her brother and unmarried incest is forbidden, and for Lot, it is that the men are his guests in the household. Both Tamar and Lot then offer an alternative to unsanctioned sexual activity; in Tamar's case, she raises the possibility that Amnon can bring his request to David and receive Tamar in a socially approved fashion, and in Lot's, he offers his daughters. His daughters. His *daughters*. To presumably suffer gang rape at the hands of the crowd of men surrounding the house.

In the history of this story's interpretation, some have claimed that Lot did the noble thing, offering his daughters to spare the strangers. This chapter is supposed to be about men, mostly (check out ch. 4 for more on family dynamics), but I have to take a moment to say that this interpretation of the story is not sufficient to support survivors. Lot is in a crisis at the moment when he makes the decision, and he does the unthinkable, which places his daughters at high risk of being abused. Yes, he protects his guests, but at a high cost. It is painful to frame his behavior here as "hospitality."

The men of Sodom reject Lot's offer of his daughters, thankfully for them, and what they say next reveals much about their intentions in initiating the rape. Genesis 19:9 reads, "But they replied, 'Stand back!' And they said, 'This fellow came here as an alien, and he would play the judge! Now we will deal worse with you than with them.'" This rejoinder to Lot speaks not of sexual desire for the strangers, and instead focuses on Lot's identity as an outsider and foreigner to Sodom. The fact that Lot then appears to take the moral high ground (regardless of the disapproval we may feel about his actions) and tell them what to do irks the men of Sodom because he is supposed to be less of a man than they are. Lot, an outsider, should not be in the position of being an alpha male and giving them directions.

Another point worth noting is that it clearly isn't "just" sex that the men are after. They refuse an opportunity to penetrate the daughters of Lot, which, as the daughters are said to be virgins, is a big deal. While some Christian interpreters have taken their abstinence from penetrating the daughters to mean that the men of Sodom are, to use their terminology, homosexual, there's much more going on here. Having sex with the daughters with their father's consent wouldn't achieve what the men are really after, which is the power to de-man another man.

Lot himself becomes the object of the men's toxic aggression with his offer of the daughters. After they promise, "Now we will deal worse with you than with them!," Lot himself is in danger of being gang-raped by the men in their insatiable desire for power: "Then they pressed hard against the man Lot, and came near the door to break it down" (v. 9). It sounds as if the men are beginning to try to force themselves on Lot, trying to rape him right outside his own home. The "pressing" Lot did to have the angelic visitors spend the night at his house has swung full circle, as the pressing of the men threatens to rob Lot of his status and manhood.

In Lot's case, divine intervention prevails. The angelic visitors pull Lot back inside the house. This strong angelic intervention is an important feature of Genesis; the power of God steps in and communicates with people at just the right time. Lot and his family flee the city, though not without some further trauma, as Lot's wife doesn't heed the instructions of the angels, looks back, and is turned to salt. Perhaps rather than lacking in faithful obedience, she recognizes the truth that we never really leave the past behind.

There's both a positive and a negative side to Lot's fate in the story as we read the Bible as and with survivors of sexualized violence. On one hand, Lot, as a man who is in peril of sexual violence, matters to God, and through the angels, God works to deliver him in the nick of time. Perhaps this deliverance isn't of much consolation, though. Deliverance (at least the immediate kind) from situations of sexualized violence doesn't appear for many characters in biblical stories—nor does it seem to materialize for most survivors, either. It doesn't seem to make sense that Lot can receive this personalized intervention when so many other people do not. This is one of many moments in reading the Bible where I do not have an answer. Lot is not more worthy of deliverance than Tamar, Dinah, the Levite's concubine (whose story we'll discuss shortly), or anyone else who has come near to sexualized violence. In fact, Lot almost subjected his own daughters to gang rape . . . and then when he's imperiled, he *still* receives divine rescue.

I actually think it's the effort to turn from homophobic readings of the text that have led to the minimization of the sexual violence in the text. That's regrettable, though understandable, as gay people have unfairly and falsely been accused of sexual "perversion." I believe that gay people *can* behave in sexually predatory ways, just as I believe that straight people *can* behave in sexually predatory ways . . . but those behaviors are not a product of a person's sexual orientation. They are a product of a person's drive to gain power over others through sexualized actions. Those of us who believe deeply in the holy creation of all people, including LGBTQ siblings, in the image of God should not be afraid to also identify sexualized violence where and when we see it in our world and even in the Bible. Identifying a person who is engaging in sexual abuse or a situation as one involving sexualized violence should not condemn an entire people group. That is both bad logic and immoral.

What's interesting (and very unfortunate) is that the sexualized violence in the story of Sodom and Gomorrah doesn't end even after God sends the fire to wipe out the sin. The daughters of Lot—the ones he offered as sexual bait to deter the rape of the angelic guests—take it upon themselves to, in turn, rape their father. Nominally, at least, this act is out of self-preservation: The older daughter says to the younger one, "Our father is old, and there is not a man on earth to come in to us after the manner of all the world. Come, let us make our father drink wine, and we will lie with him, so that we may preserve offspring through our father" (Genesis 19:31-32).

Right off the bat, I have a few questions. Is the older daughter being totally honest with her younger sister? Does she really think that *all* the men on earth have been killed? It's possible that, in the world of the story, she might be so sheltered that she doesn't realize there are other cities besides her own. However, this scenario doesn't seem likely. Would she not know, for example, about her father's uncle Abraham, with whom her father traveled, and who now lives separately? In Abraham's camp, at the very least, there are alternative sexual partners. Further, assuming the daughter does not realize the strangers are actually angels, the angels themselves would seem to represent people outside of Sodom and Gomorrah.

For these reasons, I think that the older daughter intentionally chooses to rape her father and recruits her younger sister to help her. The older sister, the leader in the plan, gets her father drunk and, with his faculties compromised, makes him sleep with her. Then she instructs the younger sister to do the same.[2]

This, I think, is supposed to be a tit-for-tat act that balances out the wrong their father did to them when he offered the daughters as a tempting sexual treat to prevent the men of Sodom from raping his guests. This decision would seem to balance out the unfairness of the story I told above, as now it is the father who made the daughters vulnerable to exploitation who gets a taste of his own medicine. It's satisfying in a way that I would rather not admit.

However, this too, then, becomes a #MeToo moment in the Sodom and Gomorrah story. Lot became an abuser (as he "nobly" sacrificed his daughters to preserve the guests), and then he too was abused. I burn with anger when we reach the point in the story where Lot offers up his daughters. I see the clever poetic justice happening here, but I still can't chuckle when Lot's daughters initiate sexualized contact with their father. I relate to the daughters, not Lot, in this story; like Absalom (2 Samuel 13), they are people whose traumatization leads them to act in ways they probably never would have planned. Their wounding, their anger, and their trauma, things which were *not* their fault, led them into a place where they *are* culpable. Their lack of power over their own circumstances led them to act secretively and hurtfully to try to empower themselves. They are relatable, and their anger is valid. Yet they are not the people we hope to become.

There's also the uncomfortable reality that the web of sexualized violence can easily catch up both "victims" and "abusers." The "abuser" in this story still should not fall victim to sexualized violence himself, even by those he has abused. The outrageously difficult claim I'm making here is that the whole point of advocacy against sexualized violence is that no one deserves to have their bodily autonomy violated. . . even people who have behaved abusively in the past.

JUDGES 19: A GANG RAPE REPRISE

The threat of sexualized violence against outsider men is repeated in Judges 19. While it's important to recognize that the main and ultimate victim of this episode is the unnamed woman, the "concubine" of the Levite man, the looming threat in this story is initially against a man. Just as in Sodom, insiders to a town view the incursion by an outsider male as an opportunity to demonstrate their superiority through rape.

Just as happened in Genesis 19, when the Levite and his concubine pass through Gibeah, where the people are members of the tribe of Benjamin, the pair states their intentions to spend the night in the square, but a concerned bystander, in this case an old man of the city, intervenes. Nevertheless, the men of the city surround the house where the pair has found lodging and make their demands:

> While they were enjoying themselves, the men of the city, a perverse lot, surrounded the house, and started pounding on the door. They said to the old man, the master of the house, "Bring out the man who came into your house, so that we may have intercourse with him." And the man, the master of the house, went out to them and said to them, "No, my brothers, do not act so wickedly. Since this man is my guest, do not do this vile thing. Here are my virgin daughter and his concubine; let me bring them out now. [Rape] them and do whatever you want to them; but against this man do not do such a vile thing." (Judges 19:22-24)

Here, unlike in Genesis 19, the tension in the story is resolved through the actual rape of a woman. Yet as in Sodom, the initial threat comes to a man who is visiting the city as an outsider. The old man who is the host of the Levite and his concubine has to go some length to demonstrate that there is a valid reason to spare the Levite from rape. The Levite, like the angel visitors of Sodom and Lot, is imperiled because his status as an outsider to the city enters him into a competition of manhood. For both the Sodomites and the Benjaminites, a way to decide the victor of this contest is the ability for a man to penetrate another man. Once again, human sexuality is weaponized to show the difference in power between insider men and outsider men.

JOSEPH AND POTIPHAR'S WIFE: A FEMALE AGGRESSOR (GENESIS 39)

Joseph is more famous for his many-colored coat, but what often goes overlooked or unmentioned is that he is also a survivor of sexualized violence. As a slave, Joseph is already considered something less than a man. In ancient times, sexual contact with slaves was often distinguished from sexual contact with a social equal; in the former case, lines could be crossed that were generally left untrespassed in society. So Joseph, sold into slavery by his brothers, is more vulnerable to sexual exploitation by more powerful people. Although he is, at the time of the story, the overseer of all that belongs to Potiphar, a captain in Pharaoh's army, Joseph is still enslaved. The fact that Potiphar is still his "master" shows that Joseph is in a position of little power. On top of that, what happens to him at the conclusion of the story reveals how tenuous his position really is as a foreigner in Egypt.

Joseph is a sexy dude, Genesis tells us. And this is what compels Potiphar's wife to come after Joseph demanding sex. "Lie with me," she says (Genesis 39:7), in a turn of phrase that echoes our earlier discussion of Amnon's words to Tamar in 2 Samuel 13. When Amnon says them, it's pretty clear what's going on: this is not a seduction; it's a *demand* for sexual contact. But Joseph is a man, and perhaps for that reason, it's taken most people longer to read this story along the lines of sexualized violence. And he's not just a man; he's a slave, and he's getting an order from his master's wife. He's damned if he does and damned if he doesn't. These are no conditions in which "consent" can occur.

In the history of Christian and Jewish interpretation of this story, this story has become an example of Joseph's sterling moral compass, that he escaped the seduction of a married woman. Joseph is virtuous and a model of purity. But all this presupposes a very precarious assumption indeed, which is that Joseph *wanted* the advances of Potiphar's wife and had to struggle against his lust in order to turn away her advances.

With the assumptions that people often make about men and men's sexuality, it's easy to read Joseph's response to Potiphar's wife merely as a statement of his own insistence on chastity. However, the position Potiphar's wife puts him in is one of sexual violation. She is exercising an unusual degree of sexual agency; for readers in the ancient world, it's as if she has become a man. Her motivations are unclear, too—what, besides sex, does she hope to get out of the situation? There's a history of interpretation of Potiphar's wife all her own, suggesting that Potiphar's wife cannot be a true woman, because she has initiated sex in this bold manner with a man. From this perspective, she is a monstrous woman, a perversion of what "true" femininity is supposed to be as she seeks to seduce Joseph.

But I don't think that is the right angle to take to criticize Potiphar's wife. Today, we (hopefully) can recognize that women are created in the image of God with divinely given agency. One way to get out of the trap of limiting masculinity that's so central to the issue of sexualized violence is to recognize the broadness of women's self-expression, as well. So the problem with Potiphar's wife is not that she initiates sex, but instead, that she expects it and feels entitled to it. Potiphar's wife is very conscious of the power dynamics of this situation and exploits them to her advantage when her character might come into question.

> One day, however, when [Joseph] went into the house to do his work, and while no one else was in the house, she caught hold of his garment, saying, "Lie with me!" But he left his garment in her hand, and fled and ran outside. When she saw that he had left his garment in her hand and had fled outside, she called out to the members of her household and said to them, "See, my husband has brought among us a Hebrew to insult us! He came in to me to lie with me, and I cried out with a loud voice; and when he heard me raise my voice and cry out, he left his garment beside me, and fled outside." Then she kept his garment by her until his master came home, and she told him the same story, saying, "The Hebrew servant, whom you have brought among us, came in to me to insult me; but as soon as I raised my voice and cried out, he left his garment beside me, and fled outside." (Genesis 39:11-18)

It might seem that I'm using this story to show how women's reports of sexualized violence aren't necessarily reliable, as here, Potiphar's wife fabricates a false report of sexualized violence against Joseph. In fact, as recently as 2018, in a high-profile national case, this is actually how people who did not believe a report of sexualized violence reacted. When Brett Kavanaugh was nominated to the U.S. Supreme Court, Christine Blasey Ford's report of sexual assault by this man came into focus. Kavanaugh's supporters invoked the story of Joseph and Potiphar's wife to show how women's reports of sexualized violence could be false and serve their own ends.

Regardless of where one stands on the political spectrum, this use of Scripture should be alarming. The relationship dynamics between Joseph and Potiphar's wife are completely ignored. Potiphar's wife is in a position of power over Joseph because, as a woman married to an important court official, she can trump him in a gender-and-enslavement hierarchy where slaves are at the bottom. Her false accusation of Joseph plays upon the knowledge that she can punish and control him even further by exploiting the threat male slaves posed to their masters. (Not coincidentally, in cultures surrounding ancient Israel, male slaves were often eunuchs to avoid the imagined peril that virile male slaves presented.) The comparison between the story of Joseph and Potiphar's wife and that of a woman risking her reputation and safety in accusing a more powerful man does not make much sense.

Instead, this reminds me of contemporary situations in which people who are more powerful *deliberately* exploit the stereotypes of less powerful people, pretending that they are a threat. Writing in the year 2020, this story makes me think of Amy Cooper, a white woman who called the police on Christian Cooper, a Black man who was birdwatching in New York City's Central Park (and no relation to Ms. Cooper). When Christian Cooper called Amy Cooper out on her refusal to leash her dog in the public park, she ended up saying, "I'm going to tell [the police] there's an African American man threatening my life." Ms. Cooper clearly knew what she was doing by making this threat: as a Black man, Mr. Cooper was at greater risk of being mistreated, if not killed, by the police. Amy Cooper knew that her story was more likely to be believed and acted upon. And she used that knowledge to deliberately endanger Mr. Cooper.[3]

Potiphar's wife knows that she can harass Joseph and get away with it. She can seek sex from him without his consent, and the peril will still be for him, not for her. She also knows that if she gets into a compromising situation, his low status as a slave and the implicit fear that slaves will violate slave masters' wives can swiftly exonerate her. Joseph, the victim and survivor of harassment, now falls from the position of relative security that he'd worked hard to achieve and ends up in prison.

SAMSON AND DELILAH: CONSENT WITHDRAWN (JUDGES 16)

One of the terrible lies about sexualized violence—as it pertains to both men and women—is that if you've consented to *part* of a sexual encounter, you've consented to the whole thing. This is one of the myths that buoy rape culture, and it's easy to see how it contributes to victim-blaming. A person who gives and then withdraws consent for sexual activity, can, in the warped logic of rape culture, be regarded as responsible for the assault they experienced.

Our culture frequently forgets to talk about how men, too, have the right to give or withhold consent from sexual acts. If a man decides at *any* point in a sexual encounter to change his mind and abstain from participating in a sexual act, he deserves to be listened to. He should not have to fear shaming, derision, or retribution. He should not even have to explain himself—unless, of course, he wants to do so.

The story of Samson and Delilah provides an opportunity to discuss male consent. Most of the time, the story of Samson doesn't get mentioned as a rape text. I personally am indebted to Susanne Scholz, author of *Sacred Witness: Rape in the Hebrew Bible*, for bringing this important passage to my attention to read in conversation with other rape texts of Scripture.[4] Most of the time, people who read the saga of Samson, which unfolds in Judges 13–16, notice Samson's impulsive behavior and tendency to resolve conflicts through violence. When he gets involved with Delilah, a "lady of the night," as her name literally suggests, we get the sense that things might not turn out so well for him—but honestly, it's a *little* hard for some of us to care—because in our eyes, Samson is an insensitive brute.

Samson is a human, though, and what happens to him is wrong. Delilah is a woman sent by the Philistine leaders to dehumanize Samson in the cruelest ways. The instructions they give her are quite suggestive of sexualized violence. In the NRSV translation of Judges 16:5 we learn, "The lords of the Philistines came to her and said to her, 'Coax him, and find out what makes his strength so great, and how we may overpower him, so that we may bind him in order to subdue him; and we will each give you eleven hundred pieces of silver.'" But that translation is definitely the PG one. The word here translated as "subdue" is none other than *'innah*, which, though it has a broad range of meanings, can well be translated as "rape," especially when used together with a verb of physical force. Here, the verbs in the rest of the sentence—*overpower* and *bind*—provide just that element of physical force that's needed to suggest that the Philistine leaders are plotting sexualized violence . . . and using Delilah as their accomplice.

So would a possible translation of verse 5 be "that we may bind him in order to rape him"? I think so. Samson is an

ethnic "Other" relative to the Philistines, and he is their enemy.
Considerable precedent in both Scripture and external ancient
sources suggests that sexualized violence was used against
men who met these qualifications in order to demean them.
Given the way the text is written, I think that the Philistines
would *love* to see playboy Samson taken down a peg—even
better if it's through sexualized violence.

Delilah doesn't make much of an effort to hide what she's
going to do, but the sequence of events plays out so that Samson may think the looming threat is just a game, maybe a bit
of BDSM play with Delilah. Delilah asks Samson, "Please tell
me what makes your strength so great, and how you could be
bound, so that one could subdue you" (v. 6). What the NRSV
translates here as "subdue," I believe we could just as legitimately translate as "rape," given the use of the word *'innah*
that I've discussed earlier. Samson does not take this threat
too seriously from the start; and from the patterning of the
text, it seems that for Samson, like many contemporary people, playful bondage may be a routine part of his consensual
sexual routine. So Samson suggests certain activities, which,
apparently, he may enjoy, to engage sexually with Delilah.
These activities, which do not actually seem to subdue or
humiliate him, fall within the range of what he is comfortable
with. First, he prevaricates, or maybe playfully says, "If they
bind me with seven fresh bowstrings that are not dried out,
then I shall become weak, and be like anyone else" (v. 7). For
Samson, there seems to be something appealing about feeling
(temporarily and through his own volition) that he is under
Delilah's power, but this is an enjoyable game for him as long
as he *can* escape if he wants to.

However, Samson's bondage games do not deter Delilah
from her intended purpose. She ups the emotional stakes by

accusing Samson of dishonesty: "You have mocked me and
told me lies; please tell me how you could be bound" (v. 10).
Notice that this time, Delilah conceals her intention more
carefully by leaving out any mention of rape or humiliation,
'innah. Still, Samson's game goes on. He doesn't give consent
for Delilah to do whatever she wants, but offers another bondage activity that is within his boundaries, this time, being tied
with new ropes.

The third time around, Delilah's frustration may be rising,
but she is careful not to show it, merely repeating the rather
manipulative phrasing of earlier: "You have mocked me and
told me lies; please tell me how you could be bound" (v. 13).
Yet again, Samson proposes a bondage activity that is acceptable to him, yet that inches closer to the truth about how his
strength can be annihilated, namely, weaving his hair with pins.
Still, Samson does not realize the full threat that awaits him.

Yet finally, on the fourth go-round, Delilah cannot contain
her frustration any longer. She increases the emotional pressure
on Samson to the extent that he can no longer avoid telling her
his secret: "How can you say, 'I love you,' when your heart is
not with me? You have mocked me three times now and have
not told me what makes your strength so great" (v. 15). Usually, the Bible doesn't include detailed reports of the complex
emotional dynamics of the characters within its pages, but this
is a moment where we get a rare insight into Samson's emotional life. Verse 16 tells us, "Finally, after she had nagged him
with her words day after day, and pestered him, he was tired
to death." This represents the full withdrawal of Samson's consent. With the emotional abuse that Delilah subjects Samson
to, Samson may *appear* to give consent for what follows, but
it is not a choice that is free and fair. In other words, it is not
really consent.

Samson's revelation of his Achilles' heel leads into the episode of sexualized violence. The irony is that his lifelong dedication to God as a nazirite is what ultimately exposes him to this exploitation: "A razor has never come upon my head; for I have been a nazirite to God from my mother's womb. If my head were shaved, then my strength would leave me; I would become weak, and be like anyone else" (v. 17). Delilah immediately takes advantage of this information to harm Samson. Having told the Philistine leaders about Samson's weakest point, she receives her wages and lures him into a false sense of security as he falls asleep upon her lap. This image of Delilah as a nurturing, motherlike figure, or at least a trusted partner with whom Samson feels safe enough to fall asleep, makes what follows even more disturbing.

After Samson falls asleep, Delilah begins to shave his head. She shaves the locks of his hair and then, the NRSV tells us, "he began to weaken" (v. 19). But this is not a translation that is closely based on the biblical Hebrew. According to the Hebrew text, a better translation would recognize that here, once again, the word *'innah* is in play. So we could better translate Judges 16:19 as "she began to humiliate him," to put it more mildly, or to express the full sense of sexualized violation that seems to be taking place here, we could read, "she began to rape him." We do not know exactly what this means in the context of the Hebrew writing. However, what is happening seems to me to be within the sexual domain, and it is against Samson's will. Samson would like to believe that here, as at other times, he can escape the playful "bondage" and continue his activities as usual: "When he awoke from his sleep, he thought, 'I will go out as at other times, and shake myself free'" (v. 20).

The physical violence against Samson escalates from here. The Philistines gouge out Samson's eyes—perhaps a cruel joke about how metaphorically "blind" he has been to the threat before him. The exploitation of Samson continues even more as the Philistines force Samson to perform for their entertainment. This was probably a common practice, for defeated enemies to perform for their conquerors; consider Psalm 137:1-3:

> By the rivers of Babylon—
>   there we sat down and there we wept
>   when we remembered Zion.
> On the willows there
>   we hung up our harps.
> For there our captors
>   asked us for songs,
> and our tormentors asked for mirth, saying,
> "Sing us one of the songs of Zion!"

Samson, who has been emotionally manipulated, sexually assaulted, and physically abused, now has to put on a show for the very people who subjected him to these torments.

But Samson finds a way to take his power back. As his hair regrows, his strength begins to return to him. With his final exertion of strength, Samson, chained to the pillars as the Philistines force him to entertain them as court fool, pulls down the entire building structure on his enemies—and himself too. While Samson's final act ends in his own demise, I find something powerful that speaks to Samson's ultimate resistance to the acts of violence that enchained him. Samson is not satisfied with superficial acts of revenge against individuals—not even against Delilah, who willingly collaborated in and carried out his abuse. Instead, Samson recognizes that *the whole house*, the whole social system, bears the blame for how he has been treated. The whole house must be brought down, and he, empowered even in the wake of his trauma, is the one to do it. Through the empowerment of the God to whom Samson prays before his effort, Samson brings down the entire house upon the head of his disempowerment and abuse.

When I teach the Samson narrative, I've found that many people are resistant to reading it as a story of sexualized violence. Samson, as a strong, wild man, does not fit our stereotypes of the type of person who is exposed to sexualized violence. Delilah, as a woman, is not someone we would typically think about as an offender. But I want us to interrogate our unwillingness to read the story in this way. If Samson assumes Delilah's request is just playful or kinky, *that is not his fault*. If he enjoys the play "binding," *that is okay*. If he finally tells the real secret to his strength (under emotional duress, I might add), the violence that happens to him is *still not his fault*.

Nor is Samson a perfect character, as we can see especially from the chapters that precede the Samson and Delilah narrative—but he should not have to be perfect in order for us to be willing to understand him as a person who underwent terrible abuse. Who among us is perfect, anyway? We *all* make mistakes. Sometimes we even grow from them and grow up. We deserve the benefit of the doubt that we are malleable people, open to the Spirit of God, as Samson is by the end of the story, and are capable of change. Regardless of who Samson has been in the past, his story merits our attention as we observe real ways in which men can and do experience abuse at the hands of both men and women.

Samson's story reminds us that survivors still have power even after they've experienced abuse. They themselves have the ability to take steps that bring down houses of violence and oppression. Hopefully, unlike Samson, we ourselves make it out from under the roof before the pillars come crashing down. Samson teaches us never to lose faith that God is still working through us, restoring our strength to do mighty acts that will set God's people free.

HEARING MALE SURVIVORS, TOO

You might be wondering why it matters that the Bible includes these stories about men. This is one area in which exclusion wouldn't be such a problem, right? It would be nice if we didn't have to worry so much about one group of people, men, facing sexualized violence. It would be nice if the Bible had fewer disturbing, gruesome stories. But as painful and challenging as these stories are, I think we need them. Male survivors need to be heard, too, and I think that seeing themselves reflected within the pages of Scripture might help provide confirmation that God has not forgotten about them, either. My goal in bringing these stories out of the shadows is to show that the pain of sexualized violence against men does not need to be a source of shame. The silence (and the silencing) that many survivors of sexualized violence have encountered does nothing but breed shame that deepens the wounds we already have.

Most importantly, God's witness to the suffering we bear does not stop on lines of gender or sexuality. The story of God's people, the covenant people whom God used and chose and led into freedom, includes the stories of men who have been sexually violated. God's purposes and goodness continue to be worked out through those who have survived sexualized violence—which is not to say that sexualized violence is intended by God, but instead is to say that *in spite* of the worst things that happen to men, God is still empowering men to work for justice, peace, and goodness in the world.

A path toward healing includes taking a look at how church contexts have defined masculinity, and how, in many cases, these overly narrow definitions reinforce the shame that male survivors of sexualized violence feel. It means reclaiming the broadness of masculinity that appears again and again in Scripture. And it means a willingness to hear what the Scriptures themselves reveal about sexualized violence against men—that it occurs, that it can be complicated, and that it thrives upon the stereotypes of "real men" as those who dominate others. These suggestions are only the beginning.

Supporting male survivors is crucial in its own right. But it's also important for the healing of female survivors. We need to recognize that sexualized violence is not just a "woman's problem." It is not a niche issue that can be left for a small segment of the population to address while everything else is business as usual. No, this is a *human* issue, bridging boundaries of gender, a consequence, sadly, of our tendencies to grab and abuse power over others. The gospel of Jesus Christ stands against sexualized violence unequivocally, regardless of the gender of the person who is affected.

4

"IF MY FATHER AND MOTHER FORSAKE ME"

Family Betrayal and Sexualized Violence

This chapter explores one of the most difficult aspects of sexualized violence to process: how families are sometimes responsible for or complicit in the abuse. Sometimes a family member commits the abuse, or sometimes families refuse to believe a survivor, or sometimes families actively participate in covering up the abuse together, or sometimes family negligence enables the abuser. Whatever the situation, this abuse represents a fundamental and traumatic betrayal that can represent as great a trauma as the abuse itself. The Bible offers us plenty of examples of family brokenness, where parents and siblings fall into patterns that perpetuate violence. While difficult to read, these examples of familial sin in Scripture remind us that when we face situations in which our families fail us, we are not alone. Claiming the parental love of God and a family of believers of our own, we can find new sources of support in our healing journey.

Family betrayal is so devastating precisely because families are so central to the ways many of us understand our Christian faith. The Bible lifts up the role of parents in particular as the nucleus of a family, respected and trusted. After all, parents appear in the Ten Commandments: "Honour thy father and thy mother," as the time-honored King James Version puts it. Many passages of Scripture compare God to a father and to a mother (for example, Psalm 103:13; Proverbs 3:11-12; 2 Corinthians 6:18, in the case of God as a father; and Hosea 11:3-4; Isaiah 42:14; 49:15, in the case of God as a mother). In many churches, the emphasis is on the family as the first and most important sphere in which religious education should take place.

I don't think there's anything inherently wrong with these ideas about families. However, for survivors of sexualized violence whose families have actively harmed them or stood in the way of their journey toward healing and hope, we need some nuance in the way we speak about families. We need to *name* the harm that families can do and have done. We need to recover the image of the family of God as a sacred community in which sexualized violence can never be tolerated and survivors are believed and supported.

The Bible is there for us when we do the work of figuring out what "family" means in the wake of sexualized violence. The Bible includes cautionary examples of how poorly families can support survivors of sexualized violence (in fact, in probably every story in the Bible where a family is involved in sexualized violence, the family falls short in some way). There's the recognition that, sometimes, the larger family of God needs to step in and love people in ways their biological family will not or cannot do. But most importantly, there's the knowledge that God can and will be to us a parent greater than the one or ones we've had.

FAMILY FAILURES IN THE OLD TESTAMENT
(GENESIS 22, JUDGES 11)

In the ancient times in which the Bible was written, the main perceived problem with sexualized violence against women was not that it harmed a woman and violated her personal autonomy. It was that it dishonored the family (namely, a woman's father and brothers) and potentially decreased the profit these men could gain from her marriage. This value system appears in the law code. It's important to clarify that we don't know how, if ever, these law codes were used in real life, or if they just represented the aspirations of the Hebrew people. Regardless, the existence of these laws indicates some of the ways that people thought about sexualized violence. This law comes from Deuteronomy 22:28-29:

> If a man meets a virgin who is not engaged, and seizes her and lies with her, and they are caught in the act, the man who lay with her shall give fifty shekels of silver to the young woman's father, and she shall become his wife. Because he violated her he shall not be permitted to divorce her as long as he lives.

Needless to say, there are a lot of problems here. No one should be obliged to marry their rapist. Period. But more fundamentally, rape is a problem here mainly because it's financially inconvenient for the victim's family. The father cannot economically benefit from the "damaged goods" of a daughter who is no longer a virgin. It's this problem, not the injustice of rape as we'd understand it today, that prompts the "solution" these verses offer. Taking a "you break it, you buy it" mindset, this law mandates that a man who "seizes and lies with" a woman pay the bride price for the virgin he has penetrated.

It feels terribly wrong that a family would ever cover up an act of sexualized violence in this way or any other way. But

it did and does happen. It feels terribly wrong that a perpetrator of sexualized violence should not be held to accountability, especially by members of one's own family. But this
happens, too. (As one example among many, we can think of
families' initiation of their daughters' involvement in the sex
trade, often under exigent economic circumstances.) It's easy
to imagine the hurt that a daughter could feel, forced into a
marriage because a man forced himself on her: "And now I
have to marry him, too?" Families were, and sadly still are,
intimately involved in exposing their own children to further
harm from sexualized violence.

While not directly concerned with sexualized violence, two
episodes in the Old Testament illustrate the vulnerability of
children to the convictions and whims of their parents. Both
Abraham and Jephthah are willing to sacrifice their own children in the name of pleasing God. In the Christian tradition,
Abraham receives commendation for his faith in being willing
to sacrifice Isaac. His ability to set Isaac upon the sacrificial
altar even foreshadows how God willingly sent Jesus to die on
the cross. God's command to Abraham to sacrifice Isaac was,
in this understanding, a test to see if Abraham had true faith.

There's something about this interpretation that feels bla-
tantly wrong to many contemporary readers, especially ones
who have survived child abuse. No child should experience
the trauma of being laid on the sacrificial altar, of seeing their
parent with a knife in their hands. A good God should never
order this. People should not have to abuse their child to prove
their faith.

Abraham's abuse of Isaac long bothered me until I found
myself in the last year of my PhD program, co-teaching Introduction to the Old Testament with my mentor, professor Dr.
Rebecca (Becky) Wright, at Sewanee: The University of the

South. In this class, I heard Becky offer the most insightful interpretation of Genesis 22 that I have come across, and what I give here echoes my learning from her class:

God's instruction to Abraham to slay Isaac on the altar *was* a test, but not the kind that people think. God's challenge to Abraham is not to sacrifice his son as a sign of his faith, but to be willing to wrestle with God . . . also as a sign of his faith. The God with whom Abraham is in relationship desires dialogue and community with humans. It's tragic that Abraham loses sight of that fact. Just a few chapters earlier, before the destruction of Sodom and Gomorrah, God makes a dramatic announcement similar to his demand that Abraham sacrifice Isaac, that the entire cities will be destroyed. In that case, Abraham pushes back against God's stated intention, asking repeatedly if the city can be spared if increasingly smaller groups of people are found to be righteous. But in Genesis 22, Abraham does not act as boldly as he does in Genesis 19:

> After these things God tested Abraham. He said to him, "Abraham!" And he said, "Here I am." He said, "Take your son, your only son Isaac, whom you love, and go to the land of Moriah, and offer him there as a burnt offering on one of the mountains that I shall show you." So Abraham rose early in the morning, saddled his donkey, and took two of his young men with him, and his son Isaac; he cut the wood for the burnt offering, and set out and went to the place in the distance that God had shown him. (Genesis 22:1-3)

Abraham does not challenge God's order to kill Isaac. He matter-of-factly goes about the preparations necessary to sacrifice his son, and without any comment on his part, heads to Mount Moriah to end his son's life.

The Genesis text presents God's intervention like this:

Then Abraham reached out his hand and took the knife
to kill his son. But the angel of the LORD called to him
from heaven, and said, "Abraham, Abraham!" And he said,
"Here I am." He said, "Do not lay your hand on the boy
or do anything to him; for now I know that you fear God,
since you have not withheld your son, your only son, from
me." (vv. 10-12)

It's possible we could take from these words that God's
intention was to test Abraham's faith, to see what was more
important to him, God or Isaac. But it's also possible that
Abraham's test was to determine whether he truly believed
that God would make a great nation out of him through Isaac.
If this promise, also delivered by God, was true, then Abraham
should never have raised the knife above Isaac and threatened
to cut off the line through which God planned to create his
people. Abraham may *fear* God, but does he truly *believe* God's
words? Does he believe in a God who will never demand an
unjust sacrifice such as a son? Does he believe in a God who
is willing to strive with humankind in the pursuit of goodness,
even when that means that humans challenge God? Abraham
has shown that his relationship with God is pure obedience,
but not necessarily the relationality that God longed for when
he created humanity.

The sacrifice of Isaac story ends there, but there's a lot that
goes unsaid. What was Isaac's relationship with Abraham like
going forward? How did Sarah react to her husband's near-
killing of their son? She dies shortly after, and no more dialogue between the married couple appears. Perhaps the shock
of the event contributes to her demise. How did Isaac cope
with the memory of his close brush with death? Many scholars
have noted that, of the patriarchs, Isaac is by far the most
passive character, seemingly unwilling to initiate new activity

in his own story. At most of the crucial points in his tale going forward, the people closest to him initiate the big moves in his life, from his father's taking responsibility for finding his wife, Rebecca, to Rebecca and son Jacob's trickery in securing Esau's rightful blessing. Perhaps Isaac lived in fear after that terrible day on Mount Moriah, afraid that any action he might take would rock the boat and endanger him further.

Isaac lives to tell the tale, but another victim of potential child sacrifice is not so lucky. The book of Judges shares the story of a young girl, the daughter of Jephthah, who happens to be at the wrong place at the wrong time. (Judges often wins the blue ribbon for the most sordid stories in the Bible!) Now, fair enough, Jephthah did not have an easy past: because Jephthah is the son of a prostitute, his half-brothers mistreat him and send him away. Jephthah is welcomed again in the community only when their situation is desperate. He is known for being a powerful warrior, and when the tribes of Israel face war against their enemies, the Ammonites, Jephthah comes to the rescue. The only reason that Jephthah agrees to fight is the promise that he will be made head of Israel. With such high stakes, Jephthah makes a terrible vow:

> And Jephthah made a vow to the LORD, and said, "If you will give the Ammonites into my hand, then whoever comes out of the doors of my house to meet me, when I return victorious from the Ammonites, shall be the LORD's, to be offered up by me as a burnt offering." (Judges 11:30-31)

In ancient lore from many different civilizations, making a vow like this is a recipe for trouble. Inevitably, the praying person makes a promise that they can't—or shouldn't—keep. It's no surprise at all that the first person who greets Jephthah after his victory is the last person he'd ever choose to sacrifice:

> Then Jephthah came to his home at Mizpah; and there was
> his daughter coming out to meet him with timbrels and
> with dancing. She was his only child; he had no son or
> daughter except her. When he saw her, he tore his clothes,
> and said, "Alas, my daughter! You have brought me very
> low; you have become the cause of great trouble to me. For
> I have opened my mouth to the LORD, and I cannot take
> back my vow." (vv. 34-35)

Unfairly, Jephthah blames his daughter: "You have brought
me very low!" How deeply this resonates with the victim-
blaming of survivors of sexualized violence! Jephthah tragically decides that his first obligation is to fulfill his vow rather
than his responsibility to his daughter. (Granted, in ancient
lore, the consequences of failing to fulfill vows to God or gods
are serious; see 1 Samuel 14 for the situation in which Saul
fails to fulfill his vow and execute Jonathan.) Jephthah does
not even take responsibility for his misguided vow. He immediately perceives the blame to lie with his daughter. And she
does not have the option to resist. Her reply signals that she is
bound by duty to be the ideal daughter, obedient both to God
and to the will of her parents:

> She said to him, "My father, if you have opened your
> mouth to the LORD, do to me according to what has gone
> out of your mouth, now that the LORD has given you ven-
> geance against your enemies, the Ammonites." And she said
> to her father, "Let this thing be done for me: Grant me two
> months, so that I may go and wander on the mountains,
> and bewail my virginity, my companions and I." (Judges
> 11:36-37)

Jephthah's daughter and her friends go to mourn what
could have been, the woman she would have become, the loss
of her future. She does not get the opportunity to decide if she

is willing to trade her life to fulfill *her father's* responsibility to his vow.

The story shies away from telling explicitly what happened to Jephthah's daughter: "At the end of two months, she returned to her father, who did with her according to the vow he had made" (v. 39). Some people soften the weight of this story by claiming that Jephthah did not actually kill his daughter, but "dedicated her to the Lord" in some way other than killing her, for example, by committing her to sacred service, in the way that Hannah dedicates Samuel in 1 Samuel 1–2. However, this interpretation seems to overlook the very explicit reference to the "vow he had made," which specifically involves a burnt offering. In my view, Jephthah blindly fulfilled his vow to God by burning his daughter.

As in other moments of horrific violence in Judges (e.g., Judges 19, in which the Levite's concubine is gang-raped by the men of Gibeah), I don't think that Judges regards this as a shining moment to emulate. Actually, the entire book of Judges builds to show how morally degenerated God's people have become . . . so much so that, despite God's ambivalent attitude toward human rulers in the Bible (after all, they're too easily idolized and can become mini gods), God ends up having to choose a king. The death of Jephthah's daughter is part of this demonstration of the sinfulness of God's people. Yet the idea that a young girl must die to make this point feels terribly wrong.

Children should not have to bear the weight of their parents' mistakes, should not be the offering sacrificed to appease God. Micah 6 beautifully illustrates how sacrificing one's children is no substitute for one's own relentless pursuit of righteousness: "Will the LORD be pleased with thousands of rams, with ten thousands of rivers of oil? Shall I give my firstborn for my transgression, the fruit of my body for the sin of my soul?" (v. 7). The prophet asks, hypothetically, if giving away his oldest child to God in the manner of material "stuff" or an animal to sacrifice would settle his responsibility to God. But the answer comes swift and clear: It is not. Only true piety pleases God: "He has told you, O mortal, what is good; and what does the LORD require of you but to do justice, and to love kindness, and to walk humbly with your God?" (v. 8)

And yet so often, especially in contexts in which sexualized violence has occurred, children *are* sacrificed along the way. The terrible choices of adults and their refusal to take responsibility for their actions render children vulnerable to even greater harm. This, I believe, is one of the ways these ancient stories *keep speaking* to the contemporary issues of sexualized violence such as child abuse.

These stories do not directly concern sexualized violence. But I include them here because I think it's important to realize how deeply rooted family failings are in the narratives of Scripture. The biological families of many characters of Scripture are deeply flawed, and in some cases are so broken that a significant degree of rupture from family is necessary before any level of forgiveness, reconciliation, or both can occur. The Bible dwells on stories of family brokenness because they are a central part of the lived experiences of many people, both in ancient times and now.

I think this is important for us to pay attention to, because so often, shame is hidden in family systems. There are stories we never tell at Thanksgiving dinner. There are stories we will never pass down to our children. Honestly, I'm surprised that some of the stories of family failures in the Bible are actually there. Yet somehow, each of these stories made it through the long canonization process (canonization simply means becoming a sacred text). The terrible family stories of Scripture are there because they are stories that are deeply true of *us*. Our families fail us. As families, we sometimes fail to protect our most vulnerable members. These stories remind us that parents and other family elders do not possess ultimate wisdom, kindness, or power. They chide us not to idolize the concept of "family."

Other episodes of family failures in the Old Testament include when fathers *knowingly* offer their daughters to men who are threatening sexual violence. The Genesis 18–19 story of Sodom and Gomorrah is one of these. As I first described in chapter 3, when the men of the town express their determination to rape the men (actually angels in disguise), Lot, the cousin of Abraham, suggests his daughters as an appropriate substitute for the men. As an extension of hospitality, Lot is "graciously" willing to sacrifice his own daughters to gang rape in order to protect his visitors. A similar situation unfolds in Judges 19, when a wandering Levite and his concubine pass the night in Gibeah. The old man who offers the pair hospitality offers both the concubine and his own daughter to the men surrounding the house who are waiting to rape the men. In the end, the daughter in this story disappears from the narrative; the Levite pulls the concubine out of the house, where she is gang-raped to death, but presumably the daughter can stay inside.

Nevertheless, the fathers in these stories failed their daughters. They used them as tokens to distract a mob of rapists, all in the name of hospitality. We should not accept that offering these women was the only way to save the men. To thwart the threat of male rape, the fathers chose this ghastly solution of their own volition and at the expense of their daughters' dignity. They showed their willingness to sacrifice even their daughters' lives, in the same way the concubine's fate in Judges 19 shows what may happen as a consequence of gang rape.

JESUS' FAMILY ETHICS

Christianity has gotten the reputation (fairly or unfairly) of being a "family values" religion. From organizations like Focus on the Family to right-wing political agendas, Christian movements and individuals have often been associated with promoting the idea that "traditional," nuclear families are a core part of Jesus' message. Well, it's a little more complicated than that. Especially for survivors of sexualized violence who have endured trauma through their families of origin, it may be comforting that Jesus invites us to take a more complex look at families.

Sexualized violence, tragically, can all too often be a reason that families choose to reject a child. Speaking up to one's family about an experience of sexualized violence can sometimes spur families who are unwilling to confront uncomfortable truths to push the person out. This rejection is nothing short of devastating, yet the courage to speak up about sexualized violence is a prophetic action in line with God's invitation for us all to live in greater wholeness. Here, it may be helpful to remember that Jesus' prophetic ministry did little to endear him to his family, either. In Mark, it's right after Jesus calls disciples that his family decides his behavior is getting out of hand, and that he's even deranged: "Then he went home; and the crowd came together again, so that they could not even eat. When his family heard it, they went out to restrain him, for people were saying, 'He has gone out of his mind'" (Mark 3:19-21). Homecoming, for Jesus, is not always a pleasant experience. His family casts doubt on his sanity when he speaks the words and does the deeds of power that God has given to him. The way that Jesus' family responds in this instance may bring up our own experiences of gaslighting, in which people committed to a certain self-serving version of a narrative try to pressure us into thinking that our own lived truths are wrong and crazy.

Jesus recognizes that faithfulness does not always look like conformation to the standards of family that society generally follows. In a rather striking (and perhaps even painful) exchange with potential disciples, it is their determination to put family duty before discipleship that disqualifies them:

> To another he said, "Follow me." But he said, "Lord, first let me go and bury my father." But Jesus said to him, "Let the dead bury their own dead; but as for you, go and proclaim the kingdom of God." Another said, "I will follow you, Lord; but let me first say farewell to those at my home." Jesus said to him, "No one who puts a hand to the plow and looks back is fit for the kingdom of God." (Luke 9:59-62)

God's kingdom comes before filial duty, even when as important a tradition as burying the dead is concerned. Discipleship for Jesus may involve breaking social taboos, such as leaving the dead unburied . . . or coming forward with our accounts of sexualized violence. The ministry of *living* to which Jesus calls us sometimes requires the dead, or those who refuse to see the inherent violence in the stories that survivors bear, to tend to themselves.

Prioritizing pursuit of the kingdom over family can be a difficult message for me to hear, especially in my role as a mother of young children. Often, I feel that my whole life and my discipleship revolve around my children's needs. But this can be a liberating message as well. Sometimes, discipleship must come first. Our knowledge of the message of the gospel must cause us to move into spaces beyond those our families occupy. Or, perhaps, there are sometimes places where our families cannot follow us, especially where sexualized violence is concerned. Our families may not be able to affirm that in order to live wholly as people created in the image of God, we need to tell our stories of abuse, even though our stories may rattle the dynamics of our family systems.

Jesus' invitation for people to follow him and to enter into discipleship extends to survivors, but just as it manifests differently for people at different stages in life, so it means something distinct for survivors. I think that for those of us who have experienced sexualized violence, Jesus' call to discipleship is one of embracing radical grace for ourselves, of denying the original lie of sexualized violence that it is the victim's fault, and of affirming that we are created beautifully and wholly in the image of God. I think that it also means a willingness to let the pain of our stories find healing and transformation in God's passionate striving for justice on this earth. I think it means the recognition that our stories are not ended by sexualized violence, and that goodness and generativity lie ahead of us on this journey still.

Sometimes, taking Jesus' hand and entering into this journey of discipleship as a survivor of sexualized violence will be more than our family members are ready to process. There are places they may not be able to go with us. Yet we press on, recognizing that Jesus asks us to move forward with our efforts at discipleship even when we go alone, without our family.

Commonly, survivors who expose abuse within their families are accused, even by their family members, of disturbing the peace and sowing discord. Conflict is not a welcomed addition to family life, even when it's aimed not at tearing down individuals, but at exposing the truth. But family systems tend to resist change; homeostasis (the state of everything stay-ing stable) is preferred over change that pushes us to grow. Regardless of the validity of survivors' concerns, the mere fact that a survivor is "making trouble" can justify ostracizing that person.

Jesus has a reputation of being a pretty mild-mannered man, peaceable and gentle. After all, he's the Prince of Peace. But we too often mistake the peace that Jesus brings for the absence of conflict. Jesus' peace comes from the hard work of reconciliation—of humans to one another, of creation to itself, and of the whole world to God. But this reconciliation didn't happen easily. Jesus died a violent death to bring together heaven and earth. As German theologian and Nazi resister Dietrich Bonhoeffer pointed out, "cheap grace" is not grace at all.

Nor was Jesus' personal life absent conflict. Jesus, bran-dishing a whip, famously turned over the tables in the temple as a protest of the infiltration of imperial power and its accom-panying economic injustice into a sacred religious setting. This story appears in all four gospels, emphasizing that despite the gospel writers' different foci, Jesus' rejection of a false and unjust peace was held in common with them all (see Matthew 21:12-17; Mark 11:15-19; Luke 19:45-48; John 2:13-16). Peace without justice was not a peace that Jesus was interested in. The Prince of Peace ushers in a unity forged only in the fires of justice.

Justice must include survivors of sexualized violence, too. We can really believe that Jesus is angry on our behalf, work-ing out justice on our behalf—even when our desire for justice, for restitution, comes at the expense of the appearance of fam-ily harmony. Jesus does not settle for a false peace for the sake of no one's feathers getting ruffled.

> Do not think that I have come to bring peace to the earth;
> I have not come to bring peace, but a sword.
>
>> For I have come to set a man against his father,
>> and a daughter against her mother,
>> and a daughter-in-law against her mother-in-law;
>> and one's foes will be members of one's own household.
>
> Whoever loves father or mother more than me is not worthy of me; and whoever loves son or daughter more than me is not worthy of me; and whoever does not take up the cross and follow me is not worthy of me. Those who find their life will lose it, and those who lose their life for my sake will find it. (Matthew 10:34-39)

These are harsh words that have felt, for many people, distant from the good news that Jesus has promised. But for me now, reading the Bible alongside survivors of sexualized violence, I think it can be good news indeed. We who have too often heard that we are "breaking our families" or "causing division" within them can recall that our higher and truer calling, beyond that to our family, is to the gospel of Jesus Christ. We cannot merely "honor our parents" or "obey our fathers and mothers" when the essence of the gospel, the kingdom of God, marked by God's justice, is at stake.

For many of us who have experienced sexualized violence, too often it has seemed that "peace" has been pushed on us ahead of our own healing or justice. Forgiveness and reconciliation are frequently the quickly offered "solutions" to our pain, especially when our abusers or the enablers of our abuse are family. "He's your brother, after all," we might hear. Or, "She did a good job raising you—you're here now!" Jesus' words about family can be profoundly healing when we realize that Jesus did *not* want peace at all costs or anticipate that family relationships could always survive the justice that God's kingdom requires.

Because it's a real possibility that relationships with family may falter along this journey. That's hard, and heartbreaking— but we cannot choose a path of discipleship, of embracing the hard and liberating truths about our world, for anyone except ourselves. Sometimes breakage with family will not be permanent. We can believe that God can work miracles in families and change hearts, minds, and lives (and I have witnessed it) . . . but in the meantime, we must continue living into the truth that sets us free (John 8:32), whether or not we walk with our families through this time.

An old favorite hymn comes to mind:

I have decided to follow Jesus.
I have decided to follow Jesus.
I have decided to follow Jesus.
No turning back, no turning back.

Though none go with me,
I still will follow.
Though none go with me,
I still will follow.
Though none go with me,
I still will follow.
No turning back, no turning back.

Ironically, though, it's often the hard decision to go a different way than one's family, to confront the sexualized violence ignored and perpetuated in a family system, that sometimes brings others into this journey. Again, let me say it loud and clear: We cannot control the actions of anyone except ourselves. We cannot force our families into choosing more life-giving behaviors with abundant "missionary love." Sometimes the only way to find healing is through extracting ourselves from our families through the most stringent means possible. However, sometimes one act of boldness is what it takes to spark someone else in the family to choose a new pattern of relationship.

Family relationships may well change, and sometimes relationships may even fracture if we choose to confront patterns of sexualized violence within our family systems. Regardless of whether those alterations are permanent, the words of Jesus can give us hope that fissures from our family, often for our own health and well-being, do not mean that "family" is something from which we are forever cut off. Family, for Jesus, is a dynamic concept that goes far beyond the narrow limits of how Western Christians normally define it. Family, in the end, means the family of God, those gathered around God's Word and who commit to discipleship.

> While he was still speaking to the crowds, his mother and his brothers were standing outside, wanting to speak to him. Someone told him, "Look, your mother and your brothers are standing outside, wanting to speak to you." But to the one who had told him this, Jesus replied, "Who is my mother, and who are my brothers?" And pointing to his disciples, he said, "Here are my mother and my brothers! For whoever does the will of my Father in heaven is my brother and sister and mother." (Matthew 12:46-50)

Jesus offers the possibility that in the kingdom of God, realized within his ministry, the concept of "family" does not adhere to the biological boundaries that we often impose upon it. Within Jesus' concept of family, what pulls people together is a common commitment to following the ways of God.

Especially within Jesus' social context, this redefinition of family is striking. Jesus grew up in a Jewish family of the ancient Mediterranean region. Family would have been *very* important. And while I don't think it's fair at all to say that Jesus rejected his family, Jesus was willing to think beyond the nuclear family—or even beyond the constraints of his own cultural group—to think about how he might draw together family.

Jesus' redefinition and broadening of family may not fit within what we think of as Christian "family values," but it can give us a lot of hope for our families as well. If our families of origin cannot accept where our discipleship takes us in our journey of survival, or if our family chooses not to abandon death-dealing paths of violence that we cannot participate in, that does not mean "family" is done for us. Our kinship comes not only from our birth, but also from the great "cloud of witnesses" (Hebrews 12:1) that buoys the journey we're taking.

Sometimes biblical scholars call the family concept that Jesus uses a "fictive kinship." I get what they're going for.[1] The family relationships Jesus is describing are not ones that are based in the traditional definitions of having a mother and a father. But at the same time (and more importantly, I'd say), there's nothing fictive about these relationships. The kinships that Jesus offers us are ones that are born of something deeper than shared DNA or a minivan the whole family drove around when we were kids; it's a birth from the water and the Spirit of God (John 3:5). We who have passed through the waters of baptism together are irrevocably bonded together as part of God's family. We owe our solidarity, our very lives, to one another.

REJECTING "BIBLICAL" JUSTIFICATION FOR MARITAL RAPE

Marriage is a crucial part of many families. This is true today and was true in the ancient world. But there's also evidence that among Jesus' early followers, plenty of people were convinced that Christians, properly speaking, would do better to avoid it.

In 1 Corinthians, Paul writes, "To the unmarried and the widows I say that it is well for them to remain unmarried as I am. But if they are not practicing self-control, they should marry. For it is better to marry than to be aflame with passion" (1 Corinthians 7:8-9). Marriage was not a given for members of the early church at all. Many early Christians would probably have been vexed by the claim that the ideal situation for a Christian person is to get married. Singleness and asceticism often went hand in hand in early Christianity. After all, many of the earliest followers of Jesus expected the second coming to happen at any time. If the world as they knew it was about to end, it didn't make too much sense to hurry and start a family!

But the New Testament writers do give some thoughts about marriage, and sex in marriage, because . . . well, it was hard to sustain a movement for too long without people getting married and having children who would grow up in the faith and in turn pass the traditions on to their own children. There are moments in these Scriptures where the suggested guidance for marriage feels quite beautiful and moving, and other times when I look at marriage in my own context and think that there are no connection points whatsoever.

And there are certain points that make me really afraid, afraid for friends I know who have grown up in Christian culture and have been in marriages that turned dangerous at some point. I have friends for whom sex has been weaponized in marriage. Christian culture hasn't done a great job of naming the reality of rape in marriage. Some have read biblical passages about sexuality in marriage and taken them to mean that it's a woman's duty to be always available for her husband. *No* isn't a valid option—so if a woman says no, and her husband insists on sexualized activities anyway, it isn't rape, it's just a husband taking what was his to begin with. If the sex is too rough, or not enjoyable after the woman has said no, according to this ideology, it's the fault of the woman who refused sex.

There could be nothing further from a Christlike approach to sex. The Christlike love to which Jesus calls us is one of self-emptying for one another—but it's also one that reverences the image of God in others *and ourselves*. Nothing about marital rape reflects this love. It sickens me to know that so many of my sisters in Christ have received such false counsel that distorts the good news of Jesus to them. So it's vitally important that we continue to wrestle with the places in our Scriptures that can suggest an imbalance of power where sexuality is concerned. One of these places in Scripture is Ephesians 5:21-24:

> Be subject to one another out of reverence for Christ.
>
> Wives, be subject to your husbands as you are to the Lord. For the husband is the head of the wife just as Christ is the head of the church, the body of which he is the Savior. Just as the church is subject to Christ, so also wives ought to be, in everything, to their husbands.

Another of these passages is 1 Corinthians 7:2-5.

> Each man should have his own wife and each woman her own husband. The husband should give to his wife her conjugal rights, and likewise the wife to her husband. For the wife does not have authority over her own body, but the husband does; likewise the husband does not have authority over his own body, but the wife does. Do not deprive one another except perhaps by agreement for a set time, to devote yourselves to prayer, and then come together again, so that Satan may not tempt you because of your lack of self-control.

Unfortunately, this passage has so often been twisted to theologically justify rape in marriage. Because of the way this passage has been interpreted, women often bear the brunt of maintaining a sexual relationship with their husbands in the marriage. Some who read this passage end up denying that women have a right to deny sex to their husbands—in which case, marital rape does not exist. Men who force their wives to have sexualized contact with them in marriage are not held accountable when people read Scripture in this way, and women are given no language to express that what is happening to them is something terrible and wrong. Women are also blamed for not satisfying their husband's desires if husbands resort to abuse in order to secure what passes as "sex." Interpretation of passages like this can cut another way as well, with women's sexual agency being denied and men being falsely characterized as the only ones with legitimate sexual desires.

I do not think either of these passages is even remotely egalitarian. The understandings of men and women and their relationship to one another in early Jewish and Christian culture are quite different from those that most people hold in the twenty-first-century world. However—and this is an important however—I still think that the use of these passages to deny the existence of marital rape is profoundly wrong and profoundly a misreading.

For one thing, this reading misses that the writers envision *mutuality* as a key aspect of marital sex. Though Ephesians 5:21-24 definitely puts emphasis on greater male power within the relationship, it still begins with "Be subject to one another out of reverence for Christ." That means that both the man and the woman need to put aside their own inclinations to self-centeredness and each work to love and serve the other. Marital rape—sexualized violence that arises from one party's selfish insistence—is incompatible with this vision of marriage.

While the passage goes on to compare the male in the relationship to Christ, and the woman to the church, this does not, to me, in any way justify the abuse of power. At the time of the writing of Ephesians, men in most situations *did* have greater power than women of the same status—as, frankly, they still do today. So perhaps the statement in Ephesians is less prescriptive (telling us what to do) than descriptive (describing the current state of things). In the ways that men have greater power than women, men are to behave in a Christlike way to women. In the way that Christ laid down his power for us, so those of us with power are to lay it down in relationship with one another.

That sense of mutuality in Ephesians 5 shows up in 1 Corinthians 7 as well. Though we may be uncomfortable with this passage's use of *authority* to talk about sexual relationships between men and women, what emerges from this passage is primarily a shared relinquishment of our bodies to one another that takes place on both sides of the relationship. As we read this passage in community together, I think it's important to emphasize that this kind of relinquishment can safely take place only within the context of a trusting, covenantal relationship. For me, I understand marriage as the relationship in which sexuality is most wholly expressed. We become free to share ourselves—to share ourselves fully—only when we are secure within a loving relationship. Given the deep emotional hold that sexual relationships exert over us, we must not use the bonds of these relationships for coercion, whether physical or emotional.

RECLAIMING GOD AS PARENT AFTER ABUSE

Sometimes, the family betrayals that we have experienced make it hard to relate to the God revealed in Scripture. After

all, the words and images of mother and father are among the
most common ways that the Bible refers to God. When our
associations to those parental roles are negative, or at least
mixed, celebrating God as a father or mother can seem to con-
nect God to an abuser or an enabler of abuse. Using Father or
Mother as a title for God can make it seem like we chose these
terms for God because fathers and mothers are the *best* people
we know in our lives. For many of us, that's simply not true,
and to dignify those who have participated in our abuse by
pinning their titles on God can be extremely painful.

It may be true that these names for God, Father and
Mother, are lost for us, and that our family trauma is too deep
at certain points in our lives (or for all our lives) to refer to
God using these words. If that's the case, that's okay. One of
the greatest beauties of Scripture is that it doesn't lock us in as
we try to approach the holy. There are *many* images of God in
Scripture, all of which, in different ways, reflect the nature of
the One we worship. Creator, Sustainer, Rock, Lover, Friend,
Light, Spirit, Word: these are but a few of the ways the Bible
gives us to look at God. It's a common idolatry of Christian
communities to choose just one or two of the many names and
images of God in Scripture and decide that *this one* is more
important than all else. Very often, we fall prey to the tendency
to create God in *our* image, rather than witnessing how we are
continually being shaped into God's. Survivors who cannot or
choose not to refer to God as a parent provide an important
witness that we cannot reduce God to these terms.

But I also want to offer the possibility that, perhaps, there's
the opportunity to recover God's parental names even in light
of family abuse. This recovery can begin in the realization
that we don't call God Mother or Father *because* mothers
and fathers are necessarily loving and nurturing. We do this

because we believe we know what a loving mother or father *should* do . . . and God can do even more than that. We call God Mother or Father because we know that when parents fail, God's love can pick up right where human love dropped off and do much more to redeem the brokenness of our lives.

This is the good news that Psalm 27:10 shares: "If my father and mother forsake me, the LORD will take me up." Isaiah 49:15 beautifully makes a similar point:

> Can a woman forget her nursing child,
> or show no compassion for the child of her womb?
> Even these may forget,
> yet I will not forget you.

The insight that Isaiah reveals is not that all parents are bad, but that, sometimes, things happen that rupture the beautiful, natural relationship that all children ought to be able to have with their parents. Family relationships are not guaranteed. And for survivors of sexualized violence, a family's failure to respond appropriately to sexualized violence can indeed feel as raw and vulnerable as a mother's failure to feed her newborn or a refusal to show compassion to her infant.

Even while Isaiah points out how families can and do fail where parents are concerned, the writer also makes sure we know that in right relationship, there's something so beautiful about parental relationships that they're worthy of comparison to God's role in our lives. Isaiah's statement is jarring because we know a mother should not forget, should never scorn her offspring. Mothers at their best are faithful, loving, and attentive. God's nature is to hold all the best qualities of mothers, yet have none of the failings.

Yet in moments when mothers fail to embody these attributes, God's nature is to continue to parent us and heal the wounds that are left by the lacks and hurts of our childhood. In Psalm 27:2-3, the psalmist accounts a time of danger, when enemies seem to be all around:

> When evildoers assail me
>   to devour my flesh—
> my adversaries and foes—
>   they shall stumble and fall.
>
> Though an army encamp against me,
>   my heart shall not fear;
> though war rise up against me,
>   yet I will be confident.

Imperiled yet confident, the psalmist's plea is for God to take on the protective and nurturing role of a parent. God's protection, in the end, becomes more significant to the psalmist than the relentless assault from adversaries and even the possibility of total parental abandonment:

> Do not turn your servant away in anger,
>   you who have been my help.
> Do not cast me off, do not forsake me,
>   O God of my salvation!
> If my father and mother forsake me,
>   the LORD will gather me up. (vv. 9-10)

In that case of parental behavior that crosses the line from "caring" to "uncaring," God can be counted on as the one who steps in to fulfill our right and just *need* for parental support. God does not reject, shame, or abandon us in fulfillment of parental responsibilities, but instead defends, accepts, and nurtures each of us as beloved children.

To receive "mother" and "father" as God's names, at times it might be necessary to name that our own parents do not model the types of behaviors or attitudes concerning our experiences of sexualized violence that a parent should. Their rejection of us, complicity, or even participation in sexualized violence means that they have fallen short of the vision of parenting expressed beautifully in Scripture. This failure might be so overarching that it occupies most of the space we have allocated for "parenthood" in our understanding. It might be hard to imagine parents who would not cause us harm in such a significant and devastating way.

The Psalms also tell us of God who is father to those who have none: "Father of orphans and protector of widows is God in his holy habitation" (Psalm 68:5). Those who did not have fathers in ancient Israel were especially vulnerable to exploitation because of their precarious economic and social position. That God is a father to these fatherless ones in particular illustrates God's role as the ultimate bringer of justice, who rights the potential wrongs that those without a father would face. This attribute of God as the guarantor of justice can be particularly important to survivors of sexualized violence who experience alienation from their fathers. Unlike fathers who participate in sexualized violence or at least tolerate it, God the Father will not rest until his children experience the full justice that they are due.

God the Father desires to give good things to his children—so much so that whatever gifts human fathers can give, even good ones pale by comparison. Matthew 7:9-11 reads, "Is there anyone among you who, if your child asks for bread, will give a stone? Or if the child asks for a fish, will give a snake? If you then, who are evil, know how to give good gifts to your children, how much more will your Father in heaven give good things to those who ask him!" Certainly (and this reality may not be fully acknowledged in the verses from Matthew here), there are fathers who are completely absent from their children's lives, and whose presence in their children's lives is wholly destructive. However, similar to Isaiah 49:15 quoted above, we know that a father *should* want to give his children things. The expectation we have that a father should do this, and the disappointment we feel when fathers do not, are valid feelings that should key us into knowing that "giving good gifts" is an essential feature of fatherhood. When human fathers do *not* give good gifts—gifts of affirmation and safety, gifts of presence and trust, gifts that all children should have from their fathers—what is missing violates something of that core nature of what it should mean to have a father. Survivors of sexualized violence who do not receive these things from their father, especially where sexualized violence is concerned, can rightfully feel a deep sense of betrayal and desire for restitution.

Unfortunately, the difficult reality is that some, though not all, father-child relationships are too deeply scarred, especially by relationship-rending issues like sexualized violence, to be repaired in this lifetime. The sadness and anger that can come from this kind of parental betrayal, this withholding or removing of what should be every child's God-given identity as "beloved," are real and can't be papered over. But at the same time, God's mercy to us is that the gifts of God do not rely on human parents' faithfulness in order to be delivered. *God's* protection, provision, and confidence in us remain constant despite the failures of fathers who neglect to give good gifts to their children.

But it might be worth it to at least entertain the idea that the God revealed in Scripture occupies the parental role with a fierceness and tenderness of love that transcends the abuse and neglect we may have experienced from our parents. It may be that there's a power in claiming God's parental love as Mother and Father, that this claim of God as our parent is the strongest indictment of abuse that we can ever give. It may take years and tears, but that might be a real healing in calling on a God who promises to *be with us* as a parent no matter what we face, and whose love never fails us or endangers us.

Therefore, when the Scriptures tell us that we are adopted into God's family, no matter the sexualized violence and other abuse that we may have experienced at our family's hands, we can rejoice. There can be a profound comfort in the knowledge that no matter what has happened with our families of origin, we are part of a family that is created through the universal parentage of God that binds us together in community. This is a foundational concept in the gospel of John: "But to all who received him, who believed in his name, he gave power to become children of God, who were born, not of blood or of the will of the flesh or of the will of man, but of God" (John 1:12-13). We can have boldness as we approach God as our parent, knowing that we are sons and daughters adopted into a family where we are beloved, treasured, and protected. It's for this reason that Paul writes, "For you did not receive a spirit of slavery to fall back into fear, but you have received a spirit of adoption. When we cry, 'Abba! Father!' it is that very Spirit bearing witness with our spirit that we are children of God" (Romans 8:15-16).

5

MOVING
BEYOND BLAME

The Bible might seem like a questionable place to turn for survivors healing from sexualized violence. After all, in many parts of Scripture, the explanation of suffering that's presented is that it's deserved punishment for sin. But the story of why suffering, including sexualized violence, happens is far more complex than a sin-leads-to-suffering formula, even within Scripture itself. This chapter shows how the Bible offers possibilities for understanding the pain we feel after trauma with more nuance. Our trauma is not our fault, and Scripture can affirm that truth.

When we experience sexualized violence, we often rehearse what happened over and over again. We may ruminate over not only the violence itself, but the events that led up to it, and what happened next. The mundane details of "the day" it happened might become endowed with new, traumatic significance. Often, the trauma we've experienced doesn't allow the memories we've had to assimilate in the ways that other memories do. It takes a lot of time, and often professional help, for assimilation to occur.

While we're ruminating over the trauma, a major question surfaces: Why did this happen to me? What caused this disastrous string of events to unfold, like dominoes that slowly tip over one by one until the whole line of tiles cascades? We may search every detail in our memories, every recollection, to find a reason why the horror happened.

For many survivors, the conclusion arrived at is this: It had to be my fault, somehow. I shouldn't have been at that party. I should have trusted my gut instinct. I shouldn't have had a beer. I shouldn't have gone back with him to his apartment. I shouldn't have stayed in the marriage. I should have said no, or said no more loudly.

There are several reasons why we might blame ourselves. For some of us, self-blame is actually a survival mechanism. If we love the person who hurt us, we may fear that the pain we will experience from blaming the perpetrator and losing the relationship is greater than the pain of the abuse itself. Blaming ourselves can also give us a sense of clarity and certainty in a time when everything feels uncertain. Lastly, self-blame can fit the narratives about sexualized violence that many of us have heard our whole lives. This moment of crisis can seem like a tough time to start something new.

After all, the reactions when we tell others about our experiences often don't help, either. They frequently confirm the self-blame we may already be experiencing. In some Christian circles, we may be told that we are sexually impure. Others may point out that our behavior was "really dumb." Some may say that our account is a slanderous attempt to ruin someone or a desperate bid for attention.

Let me say here that I think the "You may have screwed up, but there's grace!" response to survivors from many Christian leaders is as damaging as the responses of those who harshly blame. While I recognize the attempt to couch the event of sexualized violence within the gospel, we can do *so* much better. The idea that *we*, the survivors, are the main ones who need God's grace and forgiveness after an episode of sexualized violence is misguided and harmful. To say that we need grace after experiencing sexualized violence is to say that we as the survivors have somehow sinned. So we confess. Where, though, are the ones who have harmed us? Where are they kneeling down to repent of their sins? Sadly, most of them are not, nor will many of them, ever.

After all the negative feedback we hear from trusted leaders and friends in the church and other contexts, we may find ourselves thinking, *This is all my fault. I have ruined my own life.*

WHY "GET WHAT YOU DESERVE" THEOLOGY LETS US DOWN

The idea that bad things happen to us because we have done badly is an idea we come by honestly. In fact, this idea is one of many ideas within Christian tradition that deal with the *theodicy* question. Theodicy derives from the Greek words *theos* (God) and *dikē* (justice). In other words, theodicy asks the enormous question of why, if God is powerful, just, good, and all the other things we profess, bad things can still happen to us. In my opinion, the theodicy question is unsolvable by human minds—which, of course, has not stopped humans from having a go at it. But theodicy started way before Christianity did. The Bible also approaches the theodicy question in several ways. One of the Bible's main stabs at theodicy is through *Deuteronomistic theology*. The term *Deuteronomistic* can be confusing because it reminds many people of the book of Deuteronomy. Deuteronomy isn't only the name of the fifth book in the Old Testament, it also names a school of thought that appears in a much wider range of biblical material. The *Deuteronomistic history* begins in Deuteronomy and continues through Joshua, Judges, 1–2 Samuel, and 1–2 Kings.

A driving idea of the Deuteronomistic history is that people suffer because they have sinned. For example, over and over in the book of Judges, the pattern emerges: God has engaged in a covenantal relationship with Israel. But God's people rebel. That sin of rebelling brings punishment down on their heads. In other words, sin caused suffering.

If the Deuteronomistic history feels a bit too familiar to you, that may be because of its origins in the traumatic history of Israel and Judah. After the kingdom of the three great monarchs Saul, David, and Solomon was divided into a northern kingdom (Israel) and a southern kingdom (Judah), trouble started pretty quickly. The northern kingdom of Israel was overrun and dispersed by the Assyrians in 722 BCE. This represented the total annihilation of Israel and the beginning of the diaspora. The southern kingdom of Judah held out about a century and a half longer against impending foreign imperial domination, but it too eventually succumbed. Jerusalem was breached in 588 BCE and the temple was destroyed in 586 BCE. The powerful and more wealthy Judeans, including those who would go on to write Scripture, were taken into captivity. Meanwhile, the poor of the land were left to eke out a living trying to farm a devastated land.

Even biblical texts that are set *before* the exile were probably written *during* or even *after* the exile. The biblical writers had trauma narratives of their own—of their city besieged, of being taken from their homes, of seeing young children die of starvation, young men being enslaved, and young women raped. They bore the trauma of losing a homeland and becoming captives in a foreign country. That trauma emerges in the writing of Scripture as the writers hash out, through narrative, story, and song, what it still might mean for them to be God's people after all of this has happened to them.[1]

One primary narrative woven into their writing was the Deuteronomistic theology of sin leading to suffering. After all these things had happened, the people still had to make sense of why, if the Judeans were truly God's covenant people, God would seemingly permit their suffering. The answer many of them ended up giving was much like that given by many trauma survivors I've met today: It happened because we sinned. It was no one's fault but ours. We knew the Law, we knew about the covenant, but we were too disobedient and rebellious to respond. We acted like whores, going after other peoples' traditions and gods.

The reasons the Judeans would write a theology like this into their Scriptures isn't so different from our own instincts when we're victimized. We blame ourselves. My hunch is that, like us, they were desperate to have a reason to explain their suffering. They longed to believe in a God who still kept up his part of the bargain. Blaming the Babylonians was problematic because, by all accounts, the Babylonians appeared to be "blessed" by God, enjoying prosperity and cultural flourishing. Turning the blame on God, the one constant in the chaos that their culture had devolved into, may have been too painful for many.

So they looked toward themselves and eviscerated what they saw in the harshest terms they knew. Oftentimes, especially in the Prophets of the Old Testament, that meant portraying themselves—both men and women—as women who had experienced sexualized violence. This phenomenon appears in an especially graphic way in Hosea 1–2 and Ezekiel 16 and 23, portions of the Bible that deal with what scholars refer to as the "marriage metaphor." In these troubling chapters of Scripture (which, quite honestly, stack up as a few of my least favorite in the entire Bible), Israel and Judah are represented as women who have acted "promiscuously." In Hebrew, the word here is *zonah*, which different editions of the Bible read variously as "harlot," "slut," "prostitute," or "whore." These women are supposed to be married to YHWH, but their involvement in other relationships triggers YHWH's rejection of them. Their categorization as *zonah* "justifies," in the eyes of the writers, the divinely inflicted punishment they receive at the hands of their enemies. This punishment consists of sexualized violence, as well as other forms of power-based personal violence which might rightly evoke the traumatic memories of contemporary survivors of domestic violence.

As disturbing as the marriage metaphor is (and believe me, it turns my stomach every time I have to read, write, or teach about it), one feature stands out to me. The marriage metaphor represents *everyone* (male and female, people of all social statuses and walks of life) as a battered and abused woman. That says something rather profound to me about how the biblical writers viewed *themselves* in the wake of trauma. The level of humiliation they had reached and the level of hurt that they had experienced could not be expressed directly, and instead found its voice through metaphor. The most apt metaphor that the biblical writers could come up with was that of an abused woman. The language familiar from abuse—the language of self-blame—was the most apt language they could apply to their own feelings of despair and longing for certainty.

There are obviously some problems when we try to extend "get what you deserve" theology to sexualized violence. However, that doesn't mean that the Deuteronomistic theology is all wrong or all bad. Actions *do* have consequences. For instance, let's imagine that I go out and get drunk, and then insist on driving myself home. And I do so even though I know that this type of alcohol consumption is unhealthy and that driving under the influence is both dangerous and unethical, endangering not only my life but the life of others as well. Let's say, driving home, the police spot me, pull me over, and I get a DUI and spend the night in jail. Of course, this is not a fun experience for me and would even include what I understand as "suffering." Do I "deserve" this consequence? I would say that I do, absolutely! My irresponsible actions should result in the consequence that I have more limited freedom. Unfortunately, I have brought this suffering squarely on my own head. In other words, I do believe there are times when our suffering is a product of our own sin. There are moments when a Deuteronomistic theology is completely appropriate.

But, based on my thirty years of (admittedly limited) life experience and observations, I think that more times than not, the Deuteronomistic theology is, at best, *part* of the answer to why we're suffering. Let's go back to the binge drinking part of my example. What if the reason I'm trying to drown my sorrows in alcohol is because I'm processing a traumatic experience? Then my poor choices are still my responsibility, my suffering is still in part a product of those mistakes, and, I'd argue, I still should be held accountable for them, but there's more to the story. My trauma, the original source of my suffering, is shaping my bad choices, which then in turn create more suffering, and the cycle continues. Deuteronomistic theology is best used as a resource alongside the other ways the Bible gives us to approach the theodicy question.

There's certainly room for grace and forgiveness in Deuteronomistic theology. God returns again and again to rescue his people in the Deuteronomistic narrative, even though it's clear

that they've broken the covenant . . . again. Even after the ultimate "punishment" of the exile, God's mercy ultimately wins
the day. The merciful God we celebrate in the New Testament
is also at work in the Old Testament as well. Jesus doesn't
invent God's mercy, by any means.

THE BIBLE AS ONGOING, SACRED CONVERSATION

I think we often oversimplify the Bible and downplay the wisdom it holds. We say things like, "The Bible says X," and "A
Christian believes Y," but most of the time, the Bible is more
sophisticated than that. The Bible was written in different
times and places by a variety of authors. The amazing thing
is that this collection of texts eventually came together to be
canonized (collected together as a grouping of sacred texts),
though different Jewish and Christian groups recognize different parts of it to be authoritative. (Ever heard of 4 Enoch?
It's sacred scripture for some Christians!) That canonization
creates a beautiful cohesion between different parts of the
Bible. Yet sometimes those different parts are in tension or
even disagreement with each other. Sometimes, a newer biblical text might allude to or even directly quote an older text
in order to extend or reverse its meaning! Jesus himself seems
to view Scripture this way, regarding it as an ongoing conversation where ancient truths and new insights intertwine
to produce a living Word. In the Sermon on the Mount in
Matthew, Jesus employs the formula "You have heard that it
was said . . . But I say to you . . . " (Matthew 5:17-48) to show
how Scripture is not discarded, yet is woven together with
revelation from the Spirit to become applicable and alive in
new contexts as well.

That's why I think we should regard the Bible as more like a
sacred conversation than a sermon or a lecture. An impressive

word to describe this reality is *polyphonic* (*poly* = many, *phonē* = voice). The Bible is polyphonic, a many-voiced text.

Lamentations is one of the voices that the Bible brings to the conversation. As I already explored in chapter 2, Lamentations is unique among biblical texts because it features the voice of a female speaker, Daughter Zion, in the first two chapters. Most likely written soon after the fall of Jerusalem and destruction of the temple in 587/6 BCE, Lamentations speaks *from* a community of trauma survivors in the ancient world *to*, I believe, communities of survivors in our own world.

But most people don't read Lamentations aside from the familiar, comforting "Great is thy faithfulness" verse of 3:23. When I showed up at seminary at age twenty-two, I thought of myself as a devout Christian and a lifelong churchgoer. But come to find out during my first semester, I really wasn't such a Bible hotshot. During an Introduction to the Hebrew Bible class, I read Lamentations for the first time. Daughter Zion's bold, personal, and graphic account of sexual violence in Lamentations 1–2, which I discuss more generally in chapter 2, floored me. I had no idea that the Bible "allowed" survivors to bear witness about their experiences in this way. I wondered why *everyone* in churches wasn't talking about it more.

I came to realize that a big part of the reason why Daughter Zion's voice vanished was related to these questions of guilt, blame, and responsibility. Over time, interpreters of Scripture in the Western Christian tradition of which I am an heir did their upmost to erase her voice or bend it from the one of bold testimony that the Hebrew text of Lamentations evinces. Daughter Zion, essentially, gets slut-shamed. The fact she *tells about* her rape is more problematic for traditional interpreters than the rape itself. The pseudo-"Lamentations" that emerges from this determinedly victim-blaming tradition is not a resource for survivors of trauma, but instead entrenches the harmful cultural stereotypes around sexual violence.

But it doesn't have to be that way. I used to try to find ways to prove from the text that Daughter Zion did not sin *and* that her rape was not justified. I still believed that Daughter Zion did not think her rape was justified. However, I've come to have a more nuanced perspective about the idea of sin. What Daughter Zion does is far bolder than merely saying she did not sin. She willingly reveals what *she* terms her sin (regardless of whether we'd think about it in those terms) and, in the same breath, condemns the sexualized violence she has experienced.

In other words, Daughter Zion is taking part in a broader biblical conversation about sin and suffering. Yet Daughter Zion resists the Deuteronomistic theology that sin leads to suffering. One *can* have sinned and then experience suffering, yes, but there are times, she seems to argue, when the magnitude of suffering is far greater than anything we could have brought on ourselves by sinning. Let's turn to the moments in the biblical text where Daughter Zion seems to be accused of sin, either by another person or through her own words. Then we'll unpack how these instances of putting sin and suffering side by side, without the first causing the second, offer a dissident voice in the theodicy conversation.

THE BLAME QUESTION IN LAMENTATIONS

With Daughter Zion so starkly giving her testimony in certain verses of Lamentations, the moments where her "sin" comes up feel unexpected and raw. Daughter Zion's voice emerges in Lamentations in conversation with a variety of other voices; Lamentations is a particularly polyphonic book of the Bible. In the first two chapters alone, I identify at least three voices present in Lamentations: that of a narrator, the enemies of

Daughter Zion, and Daughter Zion herself. Each of these voices contains a slightly different perspective about the blame question.

The narrator kicks off the conversation in the very first verses of Lamentations. This onlooker opens the book with a beautiful poem about Daughter Zion. Most scholars agree that the narrator portrays her, on the whole, sympathetically. She is like a deposed queen, demoted from a high place of authority to a low place of *shame*. What isn't immediately clear is *why* she is in a position of humiliation and whether she deserves it. The sympathy the narrator has for Daughter Zion and the possibility of her sin stand side by side in the first verses of the book (throughout this chapter, where the text varies from NRSV, the translation is my own):

> How lonely sits the city
>   that once was full of people!
> How like a widow she has become,
>   she that was great among the nations!
> She that was a princess among the provinces
>   has become a vassal.
>
> She weeps bitterly in the night,
>   with tears on her cheeks;
> among all her lovers
>   she has no one to comfort her;
> all her friends have dealt treacherously with her,
>   they have become her enemies.
> (Lamentations 1:1-2)

In this passage, the narrator seems of two minds: Is Daughter Zion to be regarded as a figure worthy of comfort or help . . . or has she brought her suffering on her own head by having lovers? Keep in mind, the narrator's introduction to Daughter Zion assumes that readers are familiar with the marriage metaphor we discussed earlier. Daughter Zion is acting as the wife of YHWH. Here, revolutionarily, Daughter Zion is "like a widow." If she is "like a widow," then it is as if her husband is dead. As devastating as becoming a widow is today, the position of widowhood in the ancient world bore an extra social stigma and vulnerability. Women without husbands were extremely economically vulnerable, especially if they did not have adult sons to care for them. Out of the precarity of widows' situations came the laws about Levirate marriage (Leviticus 18:16; 20:21; Deuteronomy 25:5). These dictated that if a woman was widowed, her husband's next of kin would marry her in order to provide protection for his kinsman's wife and preserve his kinsman's inheritance. Any children who came out of the marriage would bear the deceased husband's name. The property passed down from the deceased husband could stay in the family. Another story that illustrates widows' vulnerable position is found in 2 Kings 4:1-7. Elisha provides assistance that empowers a widow in an economically vulnerable situation and resists the possibility of her exploitation.

So when the narrator of Lamentations introduces Daughter Zion as a widow, that image already carries with it many points of connection for the reader. But it's also making a profound theological point: If Daughter Zion is a widow and her portrayal builds off the marriage metaphor familiar from other parts of the Scriptures, then we would expect YHWH to be her husband. And YHWH is dead. Or at the very least, gone. There is no one to protect Daughter Zion from predatory individuals who will take advantage of her vulnerable situation.

All this background about Daughter Zion should reshape how we read the mention of "lovers" in verse 2. In many traditional commentaries, this word, *ahavot*, is translated in just that way. However, I'm not sure this is the best approach to take. This translation assumes that the writers of Lamentations are trying to *reinforce* the message of the marriage metaphor, rather than push back against it on any level. Yes, the root of *ahavot* is "love," but the "love" implied there is a broad term in Hebrew, spanning far beyond sexual connotations. We could just as well translate *ahavot* as "loved ones"—family or friends, without the suggestion that Daughter Zion is an unfaithful or sexually promiscuous woman.

If we remove the translation of "lovers" from verse 2, not much else in the first section of Lamentations suggests that the narrator thinks of Daughter Zion as a sinful woman. She's not being slut-shamed. The narrator regards Daughter Zion as a woman of authority to whom something terrible has happened, and there aren't clear-cut answers why.

Unfortunately, the tone changes significantly in Lamentations 1:7-9. The sympathetic tone of the narrator shifts:

> Jerusalem remembers, in the days of her rape
>   and wandering,
> all of her precious things which were in the old days.
> When her people fell into the hands of the enemy, she had
>   no helper;
> the enemies saw her; they mocked over her downfall:
>
> Jerusalem sinned a sin, therefore she has become
>   an impurity;
> all who honored her revile her, for they have seen
>   her nakedness.
> She herself groans, and turns her back.
>
> Her uncleanliness is in her skirts;
> she did not consider her progeny.
> She went down awfully;
> and she had no comforter.

The change in tone that takes place over these verses is so dramatic that I don't think it's the narrator who is talking anymore. A new speaker has jumped into the conversation, this one with a cruel, jeering tone. The clue to the speaker's identity lies near the end of verse 7. In the last line, the enemies come into view. They "see" Daughter Zion and then proceed to "mock" her downfall.

What follows in verses 8 and 9 constitutes the content of their mocking. They're some of the most graphic, cruel, and downright evil words in Lamentations. Here, the enemies say *explicitly* that Daughter Zion has sinned, and her sin gives Daughter Zion her "impurity." What they call "impurity" is closely associated with what I understand as the sexual abuse in this poem. The Hebrew *niddah* here can relate to women's menstrual bleeding. Given the context of sexualized violence present in this poem, when we read *niddah*, the impurity here might be a type of bleeding, but it could be a bleeding produced by the rape the enemies of Daughter Zion have committed. In other words, her rape and her "impurity" become, in the enemies' eyes, one and the same. According to these vicious enemies, her rape uncovers the real impurity that she had all along.

The sexualized violence actually lets other people know that Daughter Zion has sinned, so the enemies say. Even those who respected her previously now despise her. The reason for this new shame is, as the enemies claim, her "nakedness." The enemies don't say it explicitly, but as readers, we can infer that the reason Daughter Zion is naked is that she has been stripped and raped. Stripping, lifting "skirts" (see the reference to skirts in Lamentations 1:9), and exposing genitals is frequently a punishment for disobedient wives within the prophetic marriage metaphor (for example, Nahum 3:5 and Jeremiah 13:26).

As a slight caveat, I believe it's a mistake to use this passage in Lamentations to make the generalized claim that in the Bible, nakedness is universally shameful. While in contexts of sexualized violence, such as the one portrayed in Lamentations, nakedness plays a part in marking the violence that is going on, nudity is not *inherently* bad. After all, think about the garden of Eden: God creates Adam and Eve naked, and they were not ashamed (Genesis 2:25). They saw each other naked, and *knew* each other (in the conventional sense and the biblical sense), and they did not feel the urge to hide. It matters that Adam and Eve regarded their nakedness with shame only after they had sinned by aspiring to be like gods instead of living in relationship with the one God who had created them. Shame about nakedness, relational problems that arise through nakedness, are a sign of the fall of humanity. So when the enemies use Daughter Zion's "nakedness" as a sign of her shame before people, they are speaking about the fallen ways in which our world now operates, and not about God's ultimate vision for reality. This is a twisted vision of God's plan for his good humanity.

In short, the enemy's response to Daughter Zion demonstrates a limited theology of suffering: the only way to understand Daughter Zion's suffering is to refer back to her sin. In Christian interpretation, readers of the Bible have tended to take these verses as *the* definitive explanation for her suffering: Daughter Zion suffers because she is a promiscuous woman. In her rape, she got what was coming for her. I believe that in making this claim, "get what you deserve" Christian interpretation has helped shape rape culture.

The traditional Western approach to the church in reading Lamentations is flawed. It has flattened the many voices of Lamentations into a monotone, failing to recognize that the *enemies* of Daughter Zion are the one saying these horrible things about her. This is not God speaking. This is not even trusted religious leaders speaking. As Lamentations is set within the Babylonian Empire, with Babylonians coming to sack Jerusalem, I think it's safe to presume that the "enemies" represent people who are outside the belief systems and practices of the ancient Israelites. Who wants their story to be told by their enemies? The people who do not love and respect a person are perhaps some of the *least* reliable people to go to when looking for answers about moral character. Why, then, are we listening to the enemies as the ultimate source about Daughter Zion?

These words of blaming and shaming are tough to process. Words like these, couched within the book we call holy, are part of the reason why many people genuinely fear to open the Bible and go to church. When our understanding of the Bible as the Word of God means we read it as a flat, one-voiced text, we entrench the fear of the Bible that many people have. The invitation to read the Bible with each of its many voices in conversation with each other can lessen that fear. The enemies' cruel, jeering, victim-blaming words encounter challenge when Daughter Zion has the chance to speak for herself. Though still operating within in a male-dominated culture (one in which, as discussed in earlier chapters, rape was not conceptualized in the same way it is today), Daughter Zion's testimony *counts for something*. In my reading of Lamentations, it counts for a *big* something.

Deciphering Daughter Zion's meaning when she herself speaks is not an easy matter, either. She simply doesn't fit within the parameters of what I want her to say, at least not what I wanted her to say when I first began to research Daughter Zion. In her speech, the issue of blame reaches a climax in Lamentations 1:18-22. At this point in the Hebrew text, Daughter Zion has already given in devastating detail her account of the sexual assault that she experienced. She has already shown how she is a woman without comfort. At this juncture, if I were writing Lamentations, I'd place these words in her mouth: "But it was not my fault. None of it." What she actually says is something different:

> YHWH is right,
> for I have defied his mouth;
> hear, all peoples,
> and see my trouble:
> My virgins and my young men go into captivity.
>
> I called to my lovers but they deceived me;
>   my priests and elders perished in the city
>   while seeking food to revive their strength.
>
> See, O LORD, how distressed I am;
>   my stomach churns,
>   my heart is wrung within me,
>   because I have been very rebellious.
>   In the street the sword bereaves;
>   in the house it is like death.
>
> They heard how I was groaning,
>   with no one to comfort me.
> All my enemies heard of my trouble;
>   they are glad that you have done it.
> Bring on the day you have announced,
>   and let them be as I am.
>
> Let all their evil come before you and abuse them
> just as you have abused me concerning my ev-
> ery transgression;
>   for my groans are many and my heart is menstruous.

Feminist scholars of the Old Testament who share my commitments to reading the Bible with a special concern for the situation of women find these voices especially problematic. Scholars have tried to excise the mention of Daughter Zion's sin from the book in an effort to redirect attention to her suffering and abuse. But erasing *any* element of confession in the text seems to rob Daughter Zion of her voice. If I claim to stand with survivors and to empower survivors to speak, then I need to be prepared to let survivors say what they want and need to say, regardless of how uncomfortable it makes me.

Because Daughter Zion does indeed bring up what she terms "sin" in her confession. Of course, whether *we* would term what she's referring to as sin is a different question. We might ask, If women are not granted agency over their bodies, as I believe to a large degree they were not in ancient Israel, can there really be bodily sin? For now, though, I want to foreground the words of Daughter Zion herself and, regardless of our personal positions on issues like "sin," to take seriously that Daughter Zion says she's sinned.

Being a witness with survivors may mean that, sometimes, we may hear things we are deeply uncomfortable with. We may hear survivors blame themselves. I am not a mental health professional, and so my insight into these moments may be limited. However, from personal experience, I think that perhaps the most powerful thing we can do is bear witness to whatever it is that a person may be feeling in the moment we are speaking together. I believe that it's important to validate the *emotion* that's behind statements of self-blame. Dismissing the self-blame altogether, even though it's difficult to hear and even though we (hopefully) know that sexualized violence is not the survivor's fault, can feel like an invalidation of the emotion that gave rise to the statement of self-blame. Instead, validating a person's emotions might look something like this: "I hear you when you say that your assault was your fault. I hear the pain behind the words. Your pain is real and makes sense. I want to be here with you as you work through your pain. I'm also holding out the hope that one day you can believe, as I do, that your assault wasn't your fault. But even if you can't believe that right now, I'm still here for you." Too often, I think the issue of blame pushes survivors away. If survivors still feel the need to blame themselves for their assault, they still should be welcome in conversations, individually and communally, about these issues and not given up as hopeless cases.

But even beyond this point, I think Lamentations' Daughter Zion is doing something quite revolutionary by pushing us past the question of blame. Daughter Zion "confesses" sin—but she considers her "sin" as a separate issue from the suffering she experienced. In the history of interpretation, Daughter Zion's sin is usually assumed to be a sexual sin understood as promiscuity. Under the Deuteronomistic way of thinking, calling Daughter Zion's sin a sexual one makes the punishment fit the crime, so to speak. You like having sex? Great. Your enemies will force you to do the very thing you claim to like so much. (Of course, sexualized violence is not really about sex, but about power, which is just one of several problems with this way of thinking.) In these verses, though, the nature of Daughter Zion's sin goes unspecified. According to Daughter Zion, her sin is some form of disobedience to the word of God. It's *disconnected* from the rape she narrates. While she discusses her sin and her assault in nearly the same breath, one doesn't cause the other. *Daughter Zion never says directly that her sin caused her sexual assault.* What she seems to say instead is that *no sin she has committed* could have been sufficient to cause the depth of suffering that she has experienced.

Daughter Zion is bold to call down God's justice on per-petrators—even though she herself is not perfect. She need not be perfect in order for it to be right that her abusers are brought to justice. For those of us who may feel that our actions leading up to the moment in which we were hurt were not "perfect" (whatever that may mean to us), I believe this is really good news. Our outrage, our pain, our quest for justice is still holy regardless of the circumstances in which we found ourselves harmed. There is not necessarily a correspondence between our acts of sin and the suffering we now hold.

Daughter Zion boldly challenges the Deuteronomistic the-ology that sin begets suffering. She points out its seemingly inconsistent application. Daughter Zion may be guilty of something (this remains unspecified), but we *know* that her enemies are guilty of rape and murder. If sin is repaid with suf-fering, then where is the reaping of punishment for the seeds of sin the enemies have sown for themselves? It's a rhetorical question that Daughter Zion poses. The enemies are not pun-ished for their sin, at least not in Lamentations. In the book of Isaiah, especially chapter 47, the author demonstrates how the tables have turned, and the Babylonians find themselves at the receiving end of punishment. This reversal would seem to balance the scales. Lamentations doesn't include this reso-lution, though. Lamentation lets the irony dangle that certain people, in this case a woman (as is often the case in our own world), bear heavier expectations for "perfection" than others do. Daughter Zion seems to say, If God is punishing me for whatever my indiscretions are (which are certainly less weighty than rape or murder), then why aren't my enemies being held to the same standard? Her critique incisively cuts through the dou-ble standards in her situation and should lead us all to examine the uneven applications of blame in our contemporary society.

ALTERNATIVES TO BLAME

Blame works. A repeated episode in my household goes something like this: I go downstairs first thing in the morning to make breakfast. A casserole dish with leftovers has been sitting out all night on the counter instead of in the refrigerator, and its contents are now ruined. I am so frustrated, disappointed, and ashamed about the food waste that if I don't catch myself, the first emotional destination I visit will be blame. I will consider who in the home is responsible for leaving the dish out and project my feelings of frustration, disappointment, and shame onto that perceived casserole neglector. Blaming someone will feel better, will make me feel more in control than if I actually have to experience difficult emotions.

Except sometimes that narrative just isn't accurate. Sometimes the casserole neglect is a collective error. Sometimes I create a false narrative about the person I am blaming. Sometimes the person I blame is in fact responsible, but their negligence is a result of a much more significant stressor. If one of those scenarios is the case, I have to rethink. I have to reevaluate whom I'm blaming, or recognize that there may be several factors that came together in a perfect storm to cause the casserole fiasco. Blame suddenly becomes a much less helpful approach to resolve my emotional strain.

The casserole fiasco is a silly example, but in the wake of sexualized violence, I think our reactions are sometimes similar. We may have surplus feelings, regardless of whether we're able to parse them out and identify what they are. Having somebody to blame shapes those feelings into something that's easier to articulate and direct. Often, the easiest person to blame is oneself. But if we go over the whole story again, it just isn't true or fair to pile all of that blame onto ourselves. Even if we aren't yet ready to point to a single person, the perpetrator, as the main or only guilty party, we might at least be able to complexify the situation. So maybe we were drunk when the act of violence occurred. Maybe we couldn't give consent, but we didn't actively voice denial, either. The perpetrator is to blame, but the people who may have been around us and could have intervened didn't, either. The medical examiner could have provided a safer-feeling investigation, but they didn't, either. Our parents could have been a listening ear and our support system, but they may not have gotten past their own internalized messages about sexualized violence to be there for us, either. The detectives could have treated the reporter of the crime as a person to be respected and listened to, but they didn't, either. All these discrete entities played a part in entrenching our trauma. Yes, some parties in this imaginary discussion play what I'd call a more significant role than others, but at the end of the day, parceling out blame like it's deli turkey sliced and weighed at the grocery story counter doesn't really seem to do justice to the perfect storm in which we got caught. Whoever is to blame—and please hear me when I say I never think that victims are—the fact remains that a tragedy has occurred. While fingers will be pointed (and, from the perspective of obtaining justice for the victim, I believe they *should* be pointed), finger-pointing, at the end of the day, doesn't resolve the tragedy.

The nice thing about Deuteronomistic theodicy is that it yields a clear person to blame. If you're suffering, the person to blame is probably yourself or your people, because you must have sinned. If your neighbor is suffering, the person to blame is that neighbor, because your neighbor must have sinned. The suffering itself then becomes less of a question mark. We don't have to call into question our ultimate source of meaning: God himself. If every finger we point incriminates ourselves or another sufferer, we don't have to doubt God's ultimate mercy, love, or justice. Nor do we have to doubt the goodness of our fellow humans.

Trusting ourselves, trusting that our narratives about what happened to us are reliable and trustworthy, trusting that we did not mean or want or deserve to get hurt sometimes feels like a risky business. It reminds me of a wilderness area where I love to take my daughters for a walk. A few elevated stones stand in the middle of a creek, inviting, daring, someone to take a risk and step across. It feels so much safer to stand on the bank of the creek that I know and not dare explore the other side, and my daughters, at ages one and a half and three, feel the same way. They look with curiosity toward the other side of the creek, and my three-year-old might suggest, "Mommy, can we *walk* over those stones?" but both girls cling to my legs when we stand at the water's edge. One day, faced with a similar situation, the wait will be over. Daring and interest will overtake them, and they'll cautiously plant their little sandaled feet on each stone in turn. Then they'll take off to explore the other side of the creek, intoxicated with the success their courage has earned them. New possibilities, new discoveries await.

What's on the other side of the blame question for us? Why take the existential risk of considering the possibility that we are *not* to blame for the sexualized violence that came to our doorstep and, indeed, invaded our house? Is it really worth it to call into question what we thought we knew, to potentially jeopardize relationships that are beloved to us?

Only this: Our whole lives. Our lives are worth it.

We are made in the image of God. To say that *anything* we do can change that reality, stated at the very beginning of our sacred canon, is, in my mind, blasphemy. What God has made

holy is a sin to treat like trash. When we blame ourselves, what
we are suggesting is that our lives are less than holy. That our
lives can be treated like trash with impunity.

There are words from the Bible we might read that entrench
the worthless feeling we have that both leads to and emanates
from our self-blame. Lamentations might hold some of those
words for us. And there are other words we can turn to instead.

The voice of God at creation: "So God created humankind
in his image, in the image of God he created them; male and
female he created them" (Genesis 1:27).

The voice of God speaking to Jeremiah: "Before I formed
you in the womb I knew you, and before you were born I
consecrated you" (Jeremiah 1:5).

The voice of God speaking through the psalmist: "For it
was you who formed my inward parts; you knit me together
in my mother's womb. I praise you, for I am fearfully and
wonderfully made. Wonderful are your works; that I know
very well" (Psalm 139:13-14).

The voice of God at Jesus' baptism: "You are my Son, the
Beloved, with you I am well pleased" (Mark 1:11).

Our goodness means that it's *never okay and never justified* to take what God has gently, tenderly made and treat it
like rubbish. We desperately need a way to respond to sexualized violence that goes beyond blame to lament the tragic
reality that so often, what God has made and called good has
been mistreated.

AN INVITATION TO COMPLEX REALITY

If you are a survivor, and if as you come to the end of this chapter you realize that your own feelings of self-blame for your
experiences of sexualized violence remain unmoved, please
extend patience to yourself. If you can't yet say, "It wasn't

my fault," you still belong in the community of believers and survivors. Perhaps you know intellectually that nothing you could have done should have brought this horrific experience to your doorstep. Emotionally, though, that reality may not yet have set in. My prayer for you and my faith on your behalf is that one day, you will own the truth that *the grace you need is not because sin brought about your experience of violence.* The grace we need is to live in a world in which many things are beyond our control. We need a grace to walk patiently with ourselves through this process of self-reconstruction.

My invitation for you is to embrace a world of messy realities about ourselves. We are not perfect. We are made in the image of God (Genesis 1:27), and God knows us inside and out, from the time we were growing in our mother's womb (Jeremiah 1:5; Psalm 139:13). *We are made in the image of a good God.* This is not the only truth about ourselves that we need to know and hear, but I think it's the most fundamental one. All that happens after can distort or taint that reality, but it can't change it. Try as we might, humanity can't change the good things that God has made.

So when I say that humanity is also sinful or broken, I hope you hear this: *Any sin that we participate in, any brokenness that is done to us or that we inherit, does not change the truth that we are made in the image of God.* There's no degree of brokenness we can find ourselves in such that when God beholds us, Holy can't see Holy reflected back. There's no degree of sinfulness to which we can descend that God cannot redeem us. One of my favorite verses in Scripture, which is tragically underquoted, is 2 Samuel 14:14: "We must all die; we are like water spilled on the ground, which cannot be gathered up. But God will not take away a life; he will devise plans so as not to keep an outcast banished forever from his presence." This is a word of wisdom given to King David about his son Absalom, from whom he was estranged after Absalom murdered his brother Amnon, the rapist of Tamar. What moves me here is the idea that God does not give up hope. Regardless of the complexities of the stories that have brought us to this point, our lives are valuable and worth saving. God is forever devising ways to bring us back to him and to ourselves.

Our society has the mistaken idea that to be considered a "victim" worthy of compassion and justice, the person must be completely blameless. If a young, unarmed Black man has been smoking pot and then gets shot . . . well, he really shouldn't have been smoking pot. God forbid if a young Latinx teenager had shoplifted candy before being shot! If a woman has become intoxicated before her rape, or a young boy accepted baseball cards from a stranger before being molested . . . well, they can't *really* be victims of assault, because they did something questionable beforehand.

This way of thinking is completely wrongheaded. The punishment (if one "should" even exist) for smoking pot or shoplifting shouldn't be execution. The punishment for drinking alcohol or accepting favors shouldn't be sexualized violence.

On the other hand, we're often very open to hearing complex narratives about perpetrators. Andrew Jackson may have spearheaded the Indian Removal Act that led to the Trail of Tears—but, we tell ourselves, he expanded voting rights to all white men regardless of property ownership! A famous basketball star may have committed rape—but, we tell ourselves, he was a great father! A prominent senator may have groped an intern—but, we tell ourselves, he worked on issues of labor justice!

The solution is not to reduce each of us to the worst thing we have ever done or to stop seeing perpetrators as people too.

Ironically, reducing people who have committed acts of sexualized violence to this crime minimizes the tragic commonness of sexual violence. Men commit rape and then go on to be decent or even good fathers *all the time*. Women participate in sexual abuse of their children and make contributions to society *all the time*. The politicians whose legislation we support have skeletons in their closet *all the time*. Historical figures make important progress in some ways, but are completely immoral in others . . . all the time. The thing is, we *all* deserve to have a complex story told about us.

Just as there is no perfectly depraved perpetrator, so there shouldn't have to be a "perfect" victim or survivor. This is a reality that Daughter Zion beautifully illustrates through her dual "confession" and her bold statements that others' decisions are responsible for the abuse she experienced. Those of us who have lived through sexualized violence shouldn't be held to a higher standard than those who harmed us in order to be taken seriously. Romans 3:22-23 tells us, "For there is no distinction, since all have sinned and fall short of the glory of God." Not one of us has lived a perfect life up to any moment of trauma we might experience. No matter what our past has been, it does not justify the trauma we have suffered. Errors in judgment—others', our own—may have even played into the perfect storm in which we were caught on that day or night, or in that season. *But no sin committed, ever, makes sexualized violence the fault of the survivor.* We shouldn't have to feel that we must hide parts of our stories in order to be treated as people. Period.

My invitation to you is to embrace the messiness of our reality. We are people, living out narratives in which we are neither angels nor devils, but humans blessed and called "good" by God. We bear the marks of humanity's self-estrangement from

God, of the choices that others and we ourselves have made that push us toward darkness. Our imperfections, though, will never mean that sexualized violence is our fault.

GETTING THERE: RELINQUISHING SELF-BLAME

One of the scariest and most costly things we can do is refuse to shoulder the blame for what others, acting abusively, have done. I reiterate that I am not a mental health professional, and the advice I share comes purely from experience and listening to other survivors. With that said, I want to share a few ideas about what it can look like to stand in our own imperfect humanity and say, "What happened to me is not my fault. What happened to me was wrong."

First, I want to emphasize that it's rarely a one-and-done process. There may be times when we boldly renounce the violence done to us . . . and then go on to doubt that renunciation the very next day. There may even be *years* when a traumatic memory troubles us very little, and then reemerges as problematic in connection with a more contemporary event. That means we must have patience and grace for ourselves when our intellectual side knows it's not our fault but our emotional side takes time to catch up. The ability to say "It's not my fault" does not endow us with a special moral status. We're just as good and beloved in God's sight and just as welcome at the table of God's people if we have times of self-blame and doubt.

Second, shame and blame are maladies that flourish in dark shadows and corners. When we bring self-blame into the light of day within a loving community, it's less likely to spread and grow. Of course, there will be moments of betrayal, even by those we think we can trust, whose own brokenness may influence their choice to reinforce feelings of blame. We need to exercise wisdom in choosing whom we will disclose our experiences to and discuss them with.

To truly begin to move through self-blame, finding "brave spaces" in which we can tell our story, our whole story, including the parts that tempt us to blame ourselves, is crucial. Brave spaces can be especially powerful when we're convening with people whose narratives include some type of pain analogous to our own. When we hear someone else's story, it's hard to harshly judge them in the way that we, at times, judge ourselves. We might find ourselves in the act of encouraging the practice of self-love to someone else and find that we are depriving ourselves of that very kindness. If it's so clear to us that someone else's experience of sexualized violence is not *their* fault, then perhaps we're being too hard on ourselves, too. Self-blame clings, barnacle-like, to the ships we sail through life; it can't help but dissolve in communities of grace and love.

Third, it may help to relinquish our need for a *why* for every aspect of our situations. Often, self-blame arises because we need to have a reason for our suffering. Pointing the finger toward ourselves can provide that why—albeit, a painful and horrific one. The desire for control over some aspect of our narrative can be so strong that we're willing to accept the falsehood that we brought sexualized violence upon ourselves—even if the cost is our own lives. Even if we're able to recognize that the person who is actually responsible for our abuse is the abuser, the questions don't end. Why did they make this terrible choice? What brokenness in their lives marred the image of God in them such that they made this destructive decision? Is the possibility of redemption real for them, as well? How could they do this to us?

These are questions we can bring directly to God. Daughter Zion models for us how there's an alternative to blame.

We may confront God with the hardest questions we know how to ask. Granted, the response may not come readily or in the way we wanted to hear; in Lamentations, God does not respond to Daughter Zion directly within the pages of poetry. Yet I think the process of grappling, of asking unanswerable (by humans) questions, of refusing to settle for self-blaming answers that chip away at our own humanity, changes us. By asking these questions, we stand firm in our foundational beliefs that we *are* good, we *are* beloved, and we *are* a temple of the Holy Spirit.

6

JESUS AND SEXUALIZED VIOLENCE

One of the biggest questions that Christian survivors of sexualized violence and those who care about survivors may have is the relationship of Jesus' story to the experiences of sexualized violence that are represented in the Bible and today. This chapter explores aspects of Jesus' life and ministry that relate to sexualized violence, as well as how a trauma-informed perspective can shape our theological understandings of Jesus. From his conception to his life beyond the grave and in the end times, Jesus' story can be read in relation to sexualized violence. In the story and theology of Jesus, we encounter the heart of a God who stands in solidarity with survivors and in pursuit of a world free of sexualized violence.

CONFRONTING CONSENT AT THE ANNUNCIATION

I was a second-year graduate teaching assistant when somebody asked me a really good question. It was the kind of question that you hope *doesn't* come up when you're early in your teaching career and a bit unsure of your credentials. But that smart, eager student asked it anyway, pausing from furiously taking notes on her laptop to raise her hand.

"Susannah," she asked me, "did Mary have a choice when she got pregnant by the Holy Spirit? Or was Mary raped?"

Uh-oh. This would certainly not be the last time I heard this question, but the first time really took me by surprise. It (naively) had never occurred to me to think about the conception of our Lord and Savior Jesus Christ in terms of sexualized violence. Is the annunciation story more of an *announcement* of what's going to happen, regardless of Mary's opinion on the matter, or is it more of a request, like, "Please, Mary, will you do me the great honor of becoming pregnant with God's Son who will save the world?"

The annunciation story isn't exactly clear. At the beginning of the story of Luke 1:26-38, it seems like Mary's pregnancy is already a done deal. The verbs *syllēmpsē* (you will conceive), *texē* (you will bear), and *kaleseis* (you will call) are in the future indicative tense, prophesying that Jesus' unusual birth from Mary is something that will come to pass rather than merely a suggestion about a possibility. For example, verse 31 reads, "And now, you will conceive in your womb and bear a son, and you will name him Jesus." But this certainly isn't the end of the story. The angel Gabriel doesn't seem to expect that Mary will simply submit to impregnation silently or involuntarily. Mary has the opportunity to ask questions, to express her doubt. Just a few verses later, Mary voices what is a very reasonable question: "How can this be, since I am a virgin?" (v. 34). The angel doesn't react with annoyance at all, but offers, in return, a more complete explanation: "The angel said to her, 'The Holy Spirit will come upon you, and the power of the Most High will overshadow you; therefore the child to be born will be holy; he will be called Son of God. . . . For nothing will be impossible with God'" (vv. 35-37).

The encounter between Mary and the angel, and the development of Mary's pregnancy, occurs only after Mary gives her consent. It's only in verse 38 that Mary finally ends the dialogue, saying, "Here am I, the servant of the Lord; let it be with me according to your word." Mary's speech here shows a sense of command that belies her status as a very young woman. This phrase, "let it be done," is Mary's way of issuing a command, an expression of volition or *her* own will. This, for me, is the moment in which Mary gives her consent to become pregnant with Jesus.

It's only at this point, *after* Mary's consent has been obtained, that the angel feels that he has accomplished his mission. If his job were just to *tell* Mary about an inevitable fact, he could have quickly delivered his message and then left. That the angel tarries and engages in genuine conversation with Mary indicates, to me, that Mary's consent matters to God. Mary is not a survivor of rape but a woman who courageously steps into a vocation as the bearer of God and makes a choice that will doubtless expose her to ridicule and contempt as a sexually promiscuous woman.

What comes after this in Luke's gospel does even more to suggest that this is a story where Mary, empowered, makes her own choice. Mary's song of praise, often called the Magnificat in Christian tradition, celebrates the values at the heart of the gospel in Luke:

> My soul magnifies the Lord,
>   and my spirit rejoices in God my Savior,
> for he has looked with favor on the lowliness of his servant.
>   Surely, from now on all generations will call me blessed;
> for the Mighty One has done great things for me,

and holy is his name.
His mercy is for those who fear him
    from generation to generation.
He has shown strength with his arm;
    he has scattered the proud in the thoughts of their hearts.
He has brought down the powerful from their thrones,
    and lifted up the lowly;
he has filled the hungry with good things,
    and sent the rich away empty.
He has helped his servant Israel,
    in remembrance of his mercy,
according to the promise he made to our ancestors,
    to Abraham and to his descendants forever.
    (Luke 1:46-55)

I quote this beautiful passage at length because I believe it shows that for Mary, her pregnancy was a sign of her empowerment. God had not chosen a powerful person to bear Jesus into the world. God chose to uplift someone who did *not* wield considerable influence in the conventional way. The God whom Mary praises chooses with clarity and intention the "least of these," whom Jesus would later call blessed, to parent the Son of God.

From this we learn that God's estimation of importance and worthiness is often so different from our own. The accounts of those whom we'd otherwise be tempted to dismiss—including, probably, a pregnant teenage girl going around with a fiancé who is *not* the baby daddy of the child in her womb—deserve our serious attention.

The biblical accounts *don't* tell us much about what kind of backlash, if any, Mary faced from her community after her pregnancy with Jesus started to show. All we really know about is Joseph's reaction. As Mary's intended, he was (understandably) confused and hurt after his bride turned out to be pregnant. Mary's own story about what happened, that an angel came to her and told her that she was going to have a baby through the overshadowing of the Holy Spirit's power, must have seemed dubious at best. Joseph's response is very relatable. The gospel of Matthew tells the story in this way:

> When his mother Mary had been engaged to Joseph, but before they lived together, she was found to be with child from the Holy Spirit. Her husband Joseph, being a righteous man and unwilling to expose her to public disgrace, planned to dismiss her quietly. But just when he had resolved to do this, an angel of the Lord appeared to him in a dream. . . . When Joseph awoke from sleep, he did as the angel of the Lord commanded him; he took her as his wife. (Matthew 1:18-20, 24)

The sensitive circumstances under which Jesus is conceived and Mary carries him through her pregnancy necessitates God's involvement to avoid a broken engagement. When Mary's circumstances emerge, her story just doesn't seem to stack up (assuming that anybody thinks to ask her for *her* side of the story, anyway, and doesn't simply assume that she's a woman of low moral character).

Yet Mary's witness is true and authentic. Her account of how God has moved in her life is surprising and unusual, but it is indeed a testimony given to her from the Holy Spirit. Her voice should count. Her explanation should be sufficient, even though no one has heard her. It's this failure to recognize *her* side of the story (which happens to be true) that speaks deeply into the situation of so many survivors of sexualized violence who are disbelieved, minimized, ridiculed, and harassed for having the courage to share their testimony.

One of the gifts that the gospel narratives give us, among many others, is a deep commitment to taking the stories of women seriously. Regardless of what anybody else might have been saying about her, Mary's account of her pregnancy was *right*. Though the disciples question the woman who anoints Jesus' feet, Jesus announces that what she has done is *right* and a "beautiful thing," prophetically announcing Jesus' upcoming death and burial (Matthew 26:10, my translation). Mary Magdalene, whom Jesus himself commissions, is the first preacher of the resurrection in John 20:18, revealing the high degree of confidence that Jesus has in her veracity, despite whatever the other disciples may think.

Like the women of the Gospels, often questioned and doubted but ultimately vindicated, survivors face an uncertain future when they tell the stories of the deepest truths of their lived experiences. And yet, in Scripture, we can find the reassurance that God stands with those whose accounts lie on the margins of what society deems acceptable. With Mary, we can sing, "Surely, from now on all generations will call me blessed; for the Mighty One has done great things for me, and holy is his name."

JESUS, ATTENDING TO THE MARGINALIZED

Jesus sets a crucial precedent of recognizing that the dominant narrative of what's going on in a particular scenario doesn't necessarily reflect the full reality. For survivors of sexualized violence who are accustomed to being told that their stories are false and that their experiences don't count, this is a crucial aspect of his ministry. Jesus simultaneously holds a certain perspective and life experience based on his human social location while many times revealing his divine nature by acknowledging other people's deep needs and desires, much to the surprise of those around him. Sometimes Jesus' willingness to encounter people in this way stands directly in contrast with his culture's norms. In John 8:1-11, when a woman who has been—supposedly—caught in adultery appears involuntarily before Jesus, Jesus' response is *not* to assume that the narrative that others are telling about her is true. His approach, instead, is to practice mercy and nonjudgmental presence. The purpose of the leaders who insist on dragging the woman before Jesus and the other spectators is to humiliate her. Jesus refuses to engage in this kind of behavior. Perhaps Jesus recalls from Deuteronomy 22:23-24 that a woman who is "seized and lain with" (my translation) in a city can be killed for adultery along with the man who commits this offense.

By the leaders' design, Jesus seems to be caught in a tight spot. If he exercises mercy, he can be accused of overstepping the law—a law which Jesus himself declares to observe as a faithful Jew. But if he refuses to intervene, something else about Jesus' character seems to come into question. Jesus, a friend of the outcast and an ally of women who also dines with sinners, will no longer appear to be the person his acts and message claim that he is.

There's a problem, though: no one has asked where the equally adulterous man is. This is not about the act of adultery itself (if truly it was adultery and not something more sinister) and achieving social resolution through whatever the normal means were. This was about associating Jesus' reputation with that of a presumedly promiscuous woman. Perhaps the leaders bring this woman to Jesus to remind him of the rumors of his own birth and to make sure he doesn't get too high and mighty. I can imagine these leaders' actions implied, "Look at this woman! She's a whore, no better than your own mother."

Jesus' words do not directly respond to the accusations of adultery, true or false. He will not convince them to change their narrative. What he does, though, is perhaps even more

powerful: He finds a way to make each of the woman's accus-
ers view their own narrative as if *they* were the ones standing
before a stone-armed crowd. "Let anyone among you who is
without sin be the first to throw a stone at her," he says in John
8:7. The whole crowd leaves. Apparently no one, whatever
they have done or not done, wants their life story examined.

And Jesus and the woman are left alone. Jesus is kneeling
on the ground as this whole scene unfolds, we know, because
it's only after everyone has dispersed that he stands up. This
image of Jesus, on the ground, below the eye level of all the
onlookers, speaks volumes about his relationship to power.
Jesus does not react by trying to puff himself up to be the most
impressive person in a space. He kneels, as he will do later
before his own death, to wash the disciples' feet.

It is only when Jesus and the woman are alone that Jesus
speaks directly to her. Regardless of her story and how she came
to be at that unfortunate scene on that day, Jesus' response is
not to rebuke her or humiliate her. Jesus' words are not of
condemnation, but of love. "Woman, where are they? Has no
one condemned you?" he asks (John 8:10). Jesus wishes for
the woman to see and acknowledge for herself that she has
not been judged guilty of any crime, adultery included. "No
one, sir," she replies, perhaps unable to believe that the angry
assembly that had been present just a few moments earlier
is no longer in evidence. This moment is crucial; through his
question, Jesus empowers the woman to become, once again,
the subject of her own narrative, a story which she now has
the space to tell with her own words. "Neither do I condemn
you," Jesus says. "Go your own way, and from now on do not
sin again" (v. 11). Here, Jesus' words do *not* suggest to me that
Jesus is issuing an undue degree of blame to the woman. These
are among Jesus' standard parting words to others who are

not, as far as we know, accused of any particular wrongdoing. This includes his words to the man waiting for healing by the pool of Bethsaida (John 5:1-15)—where we have not been told anything about this man's backstory at all. The instruction to turn away from sin is not directly connected to the circumstances a person is in, but rather is an invitation to a greater wholeness of life.

So in the story of the woman "caught in adultery" (however dubious these allegations, and however much they may summon for us the problematic Deuteronomic rape laws), Jesus reveals his risky stance of solidarity with people on the margins of society. Jesus does not assume that the dominant narrative *being* told about a person's life is the narrative that person would tell. These elements of Jesus' ministry—his solidarity with survivors and his willingness to have a healthy amount of suspicion about the "right" narrative"—help make Jesus a trustworthy figure for survivors of sexualized violence.

Another story that reinforces Jesus' solidarity with survivors appears in each of the synoptic gospels (Matthew 9:20-22; Mark 5:25-34; Luke 8:43-48). The woman, we are told, has an "issue of blood" (*haimorroousa*); she has been bleeding for twelve years. Unlike others who boldly approach Jesus and ask for help, the woman apparently does not feel that she is worthy to claim Jesus' attention at all; she covertly comes behind Jesus and touches the hem of his cloak. Just his garment, not his skin, she believes, will be enough for her; she likely does not want to make him ceremonially unclean from direct contact with her. In ancient Hebrew thought, blood, as one of the life-giving fluids of the human body, straddled the line between life and death, and coming into contact with it could therefore make a person ritually unclean until they were able to do the proper cleansing.

Very often, interpreters have understood the woman as someone who is experiencing gynecological health issues. Her bleeding could be nonstop menstruation over a period of twelve years. But for some survivors of sexualized violence whom I have known, this story comes to signify even more. They take the issue of blood that the woman has as evocative of much more, speaking to her suffering as a survivor of sexualized violence. As a dear friend of mine wrote in a midrash (a creative retelling of the story that expands on points left mysterious in the writing), "I bled the tears I could not cry." For my friend, and for others who have come to regard the story in this way, the "uncleanliness" of the woman's nonstop bleeding reflects the "uncleanliness" that many survivors feel after events of sexualized violence. For many survivors, like the woman in the story, there's a feeling of "untouchability" that comes from this sense of uncleanliness. Survivors can, at times, feel that we should not touch others in order to avoid making *them* untouchable, and to reject touch, even kind and loving touch, because of the crushing sense of unworthiness that can overtake us.

It would have been easy for Jesus to let the moment pass—after all, in the gospel narratives, he's on his way somewhere else, to help a person who, in the eyes of the world, is more important than a random woman who can't control the bleeding from her private parts. But Jesus does not let her slip away unnoticed. He insists on finding out who it was who touched him, for he has felt power go out of him. The woman is terrified, because she is not used to being the center of a crowd's attention. Her shame has forced her into the shadows for more than a decade, and so, Luke tells us, she comes out trembling. Jesus addresses her with love, kindness, and attention. "Daughter, your faith has made you well; go in peace," he says in Luke 8:48.

What's missing from this passage is striking. Although the woman has an issue of blood, Jesus does *not* tell the woman to go cleanse herself or see the priest. What she needs to receive is simply God's peace: a peace that is more than the absence of conflict, a peace that includes the presence of full wellness that will change her life and draw her back into the community of God's people once again. The tenuous step that the woman took in touching the hem of Jesus' garment may be all she has to give in this moment. Jesus accepts that this gesture is enough to indicate her desire for full healing and community embrace.

So many of us are afraid, like the woman, to come out of the shadows, to receive touch that heals us, to really be seen. I want to challenge us to take that chance to receive the love that we need to heal. We do not always have to be bold in pursuit of the healing we seek (though boldness is welcome in God's presence, God also welcomes us in our timidity). We are worthy to be touched. We are worthy to receive love. We are worthy to hear Christ's blessing, "Go in peace."

JESUS, ABUSED IN THE PASSION NARRATIVE

One of the most important Christian beliefs is that Jesus was fully God and fully human. Fully God, Jesus did things and *was* things that ordinary humans don't do and aren't, such as being conceived by the Holy Spirit, turning water into wine, healing the sick, knowing the thoughts of people's hearts, and being raised from the dead, just to name a few. Often, I think Christian churches celebrate the "fully God" part of that statement without interrogating the "fully human" part. Did Jesus get constipated sometimes? Did he ever feel desire for another person? When he was on the cross, did he really believe that God had forsaken him?

In Christian traditions, one of the verses from the Old Testament that have been used to talk about Jesus' identity is Isaiah 53:4. This verse reads,

> Surely he has borne our infirmities
>   and carried our diseases;
> yet we accounted him stricken,
>   struck down by God, and afflicted.

In the Hebrew text, the verse is referring to the "suffering servant," a special figure with a divinely appointed mission to help lead God's people out of trouble. The Hebrew text itself doesn't identify who this person will be. But in Christian interpretation of this verse, it's usually taken to be a prophecy of Jesus himself.

Some biblical scholars would say that this line of interpretation is a form of supersessionism—that is, that Christianity replaces and erases Judaism. Supersessionism in Christianity presents problems for modern believers and, to name two particularly heinous examples, contributed to violence against Jews during the Crusades and the Holocaust. The thinking behind supersessionism can end up going like this: (1) the New Testament fulfills the Old Testament; (2) Jesus replaces the Old Testament; (3) Christianity replaces Judaism; (4) Christians replace Jews. It's easy to see how this line of thinking can become dangerous.

What I'm trying to say is distinct from supersessionism. I know that we don't *have* to read Isaiah 53:4 as a prophecy about Jesus . . . and there are compelling reasons to consider alternatives. But along with Christian communities over time, we can *choose* to read the verse as a statement about who Jesus will be and how he will heal us while remembering there are other possibilities for interpretation.

"Afflicted" is the word a lot of translations like to use when the word in question is the Hebrew root 'innah. It's true that 'innah can mean a lot of things . . . but since it's used specifically for rape in the Old Testament, it's hard (at least for me) to read that word and *not* think about Dinah. About Tamar. About the Levite's concubine. And the more I study, think, and pray, the more difficult it becomes for me to see 'innah and ignore the connection to Jesus Christ himself.

We could legitimately translate this verse of Scripture as the following:

> Surely he has borne our infirmities
>   and carried our diseases;
> yet we accounted him stricken,
>   struck down by God, and raped.

I've never seen this verse translated like that. Why? Why is it so hard for Christians, myself included, to consider Jesus a survivor of sexual violence? What is it about Jesus that, in our tradition, makes him sexually untouchable? What are we missing out on if we don't think about Jesus in this way?

The fact that the story of Jesus' passion is *not* usually read as an abuse narrative says much about the blindness our culture, as a whole, has toward victimization of males. Jesus is stripped by the soldiers multiple times, first of his own clothes, and then of the purple, regal cloak they mockingly put on him (Mark 15:17, 20). Jesus is stripped again before he is crucified in Mark 15:24. In the process, and likely naked, Jesus is flogged (Matthew 27:26). Ultimately, he is hung naked on the cross to die. The humiliation of the cross itself is compounded by the humiliation that the voyeurism of Jesus' mockers, who can behold his nakedness hung up for all the world to see. Physical pain and sexual abuse intertwine as the powers and

principalities of the world skillfully find ways to kill Jesus in
the most humiliating way possible.

I really and truly believe the gospel offers beautiful, trans-
formative hope for everyone. I also believe that we miss
opportunities to identify and teach the relevance of the gospel
for survivors of sexual violence. The story of Jesus' abuse on
the cross offers healing and hope to all people, but survivors
especially. First, for male survivors specifically, I think the fact
that Jesus, incarnate as a human man, experienced sexual violence holds significance. In Christian tradition, Jesus has often
been presented as a warrior or a superhero. In many portraits,
there's no other way to say it: Jesus is buff. These super manly
images are not the *only* way to think about Jesus, but I don't
think it's necessary to discard them even as we dig into how
Jesus also presents himself with a maternal side. In fact, I think
it's more powerful to hold on to the image of Jesus with super-
natural powers as we consider how Jesus also experienced
sexual abuse.[1] The Gospels present Jesus as a miracle worker,
a man among men, a person with superpowers (walking on
water, anyone?), *and* they also show him as a man who died
after a prolonged episode of sexual abuse. No one would dare
say Jesus is less than a man. The Scriptures' portrayal of Jesus
as abused on the cross invites us toward an understanding
that real, vibrant, and dynamic masculinity can encompass the
deepest hurts people can bear.

Second, Jesus' experience of sexual abuse reminds all of us
that God in Christ is with us in whatever kind of suffering our
stories hold. God does not hang out in heaven, detached from
the wrongful abuse that we can experience, but instead enters
human brokenness in some of the most profound ways possible, even enduring sexual abuse. When we find ourselves broken, abused, humiliated, and tortured, we can know that God

in Christ can relate to us. We are never, ever alone, because in Jesus' life, God bears witness that sexual violence is one of the most heinous evils that can happen to a person.

JESUS' ABUSE: A NECESSARY EVIL?

There are many powerful and positive ways that reading Jesus as a survivor of sexual violence can influence us. But there are also valid questions we need to ask. If Jesus suffered sexual abuse and he died to free us from the powers of sin and death, does that mean that sexual abuse can sometimes be a necessary evil on the way to a greater purpose? If Jesus went willingly to the cross, does that mean that he brought this abuse upon himself?

Sexual violence is not a "necessary evil" . . . not in Jesus' life, and not in our lives either. Jesus' abuse dramatically reveals what happens when God's perfect love comes into contact with the sinfulness of the world. Jesus, as fully as he was human, as fully as he bore all our suffering, had a knowledge and a grace that none of us can have . . . because he was fully God as well. So as he anticipates his forthcoming suffering and death, he has an insight into what will happen to him that goes beyond what any of the rest of us could. The Gospels show the tension in Jesus' humanity and divinity as they give different stories about what it was like for Jesus as he anticipated the terrible events on the Friday we'd eventually call "Good." In Mark, Jesus appears to struggle with God as he prays, bringing to mind Jacob wrestling with the angel in Genesis 32. Jesus begs for the cup to pass from him if there is any other way. But in John, Jesus seems fully in control of himself and the situation, praying (with acceptance, it seems), "Father, the hour has come; glorify your Son so that the Son may glorify you" (17:1). And then Jesus segues into a long prayer that seems only a little bit related to the fact that he's about to be crucified! The gospel writers are trying to tell rather different stories about who Jesus was and what his life and death would mean. Mark especially wants us to know that Jesus was a *human*, that his suffering was real and emotional and bodily. John doesn't want us to forget that Jesus was *God*, powerful and with the full knowledge of God.

We need both narratives. I don't think one is "right" and the other "wrong." Instead, together, we get a fuller picture of the amazing revelation of God that became incarnate in Jesus Christ. And both narratives help us grapple with the tough questions of how we relate to Jesus as a survivor of sexual violence.

Another question that comes out of Jesus' crucifixion is this: Can we fully trust a God who allows such terrible abuse and pain to happen to his own Son? Is this a God who, approached as a parent, will reawaken the family wounds that so many of us bear? Would a good God devise such a violent path for the reconciliation of the world to God's own heart? The only way I can find through these questions is the most profound identification of God the Father, Creator, Parent (whatever language feels most right to us) with the cross itself. The suffering of Jesus the Son is shared wholly by God, who does not inflict this sexualized crucifixion on an outside entity, but experiences it radically within his own being.

RISEN WITH SCARS

If the crucifixion includes sexualized violence, among other evils, then our understanding of the resurrection suggests that something about the dominant role of sexualized violence in our world has been forever shaken. Sexualized violence is part of the process toward Jesus' death . . . but Jesus does not stay dead. One of the absurd yet most profound proclamations of Christianity is that Jesus, human in his death, is raised from the dead.

This proclamation seemed no less absurd to the people who loved Jesus then, back in the early years of the Common Era, than it does to us now, some two thousand years later. The first witnesses to the resurrection in the Gospels are women. (This detail in the story is something that gives infinite satisfaction to those of us who are invested in making the claim that not only men, but also women, were members of Jesus' intimate circle of followers.) It's ironic, really, that the first preachers of the resurrection are women, because this fact makes the astounding and incredible truth of Jesus' new life even more difficult for the male disciples of Jesus to accept. Then, as now, women's testimony could sometimes count for little.

In the gospel of John, this is especially true for Thomas, one of Jesus' disciples who misses both the initial discovery of the empty tomb and Jesus' subsequent visit to the disciples who fearfully waited in a locked room. Thomas insists that he needs evidence to believe that Jesus truly has been raised from the dead: "Unless I see the mark of the nails in his hands, and put my finger in the mark of the nails and my hand in his side, I will not believe" (John 20:25).

Thomas's insistence on seeing in the flesh a real, raised Christ makes a lot of sense. Thomas, with the other disciples, has borne witness to Jesus' suffering and death. He himself is still reeling from the trauma of Jesus' abuse. (Recall that trauma affects us not only when we ourselves experience a traumatic event, but also when someone we love experiences a trauma.) Thomas has internalized the reality of Jesus' suffering. He—to his credit!—does not want to minimize it or make light of it by pretending it can all be wished away by a magic

trick. Thomas, we can see, is someone who takes suffering
seriously. Many people who are trying to become allies of survivors of sexualized violence would do well to learn from his
lesson. We cannot expect healing to come quickly or facilely.

Jesus walks the difficult line that Thomas needs of demon-
strating the reality of the resurrection while also showing that
the trauma of the past does not simply dissolve; it leaves marks
on us. At Jesus' next appearance to the disciples, Thomas is
present, and Jesus meets Thomas's need to witness that the
resurrection message does not simply mock or erase the past.
Jesus says to him, "Put your finger here and see my hands.
Reach out your hand and put it in my side. Do not doubt but
believe" (v. 27).

If we understand the cross as, among other things, representing Jesus' encounter with sexualized violence, the resurrection should, among other things, represent how Jesus' healing
process takes place. It would be easy to claim that Jesus' resurrection completely erases the pain of the past and gives him
a completely clean slate to begin his post-cross life. But the
reality is more complicated than that. Jesus still has scars after
he is raised from the dead. The new life that he receives does
not erase the memory of the past. Jesus does not go on after
the cross and the tomb in the same way he did before them.

This can speak to those of us who are struggling to figure
out what healing looks like in our own lives. So often, we are
rushed to "move on" or "recover." Often, these well-meaning
but flawed admonitions seem like they come at the expense of
the authenticity of our lived experience. What has happened
has changed us forever. We don't want to deny that our testimony is real and valid, that it really happened, and that it has
formed parts of who we are. If it means forgetting or denying,
we can't just "move on."

Jesus' resurrection invites us into a different way of inter-
acting with the trauma of our past. Neither the pain of the
cross nor the victory of the empty tomb stands alone at the end
of the Gospels. Jesus' body bears the memory of his trauma
through scars that are available for anyone to see and touch.
The pain of his past is real and legitimate. Yet the scars on his
body do not undermine the fact that *he is alive.* His new life
comes through and along with the scars his body bears, and
they tell the story that new life has passed through the pain
of the past and bears witness to all the struggle that has come
before. The resurrection does not mean that our stories and
scars cease to matter, but rather declares that the power of
goodness and love define the ending.

The resurrection stands in defiance to the people, systems
of oppression, and circumstances that claim to have ultimate
power over us through inflicting sexualized violence. Each of
us, no matter the pain in our stories that has placed us in a
tomb, has access to the mighty power of God that raised Jesus
from the dead. The New Testament gives us the supreme hope
that we too will share in Christ's resurrection. Even the pain
of sexualized violence, part of the journey to Jesus' death and
an experience which so many of us share, will not leave us
alienated from God's life-giving power. Romans 6:5 tells us,
"For if we have been united with him in a death like his, we
will certainly be united with him in a resurrection like his."
Traditionally, Christians believe Jesus descended into hell
during the days that he was dead. We may feel that we too are
on the road to hell in the process toward resurrection, but we
can rest assured that God's healing and reconciling work in
our lives is not done.

Romans 8:11 assures us that the power that was so strong
in Jesus' life, strong enough to raise him from the dead, is

ours to receive as well: "If the Spirit of him who raised Jesus from the dead dwells in you, he who raised Christ from the dead will give life to your mortal bodies also through his Spirit that dwells in you." As we witness Jesus overcoming the grave and the trauma that the road to his death held for him, we can be assured that victory over evil is possible for us as well. Sexualized violence is not the end of our story, but neither do we have to forget it or pretend that it does not exist. The power of God to restore us to health and wholeness comes not at the expense of the authenticity and truth of our story, but through it. Our scars don't vanish, but rather give testimony to the power of God to strengthen us and redeem our lives even in the most difficult circumstances. The grave could not hold Jesus. The grave cannot hold us.

IMAGINING CHRIST'S REIGN: GRAPPLING WITH VIOLENT IMAGERY IN REVELATION

I think most of us want to have a vision of the end of all things that includes healing, restoration, unity among God's people, and full restoration of God's people to God's self. The Jesus we celebrate, the Prince of Peace, seems to come as the consummation of the best things for the world that we can possibly imagine. But anyone who has read the book of Revelation knows that the portrait painted by John's apocalyptic visions is sometimes anything but idyllic. In prophesying against the church in Thyatira, John writes that the Son of Man says,

> But I have this against you: you tolerate that woman Jezebel, who calls herself a prophet and is teaching and beguiling my servants to practice fornication and to eat food sacrificed to idols. I gave her time to repent, but she refuses to repent of her fornication. Beware, I am throwing her

on a bed, and those who commit adultery with her I am throwing into great distress, unless they repent of her doings. (Revelation 2:20-22)

In Revelation 17:16, another figure of a woman also experiences sexualized violence as she experiences what is understood as her apocalyptic punishment. These passages closely recall the personification of cities as women in the Bible, where the catastrophic fate of either Israel or another adversarial people meets the wrath of God as a husband. This woman is described as a "prostitute" who has had sexual relations with the kings of the earth, and she rides on a great beast. While in the Revelation text, the explicit entity associated with the woman is Babylon, in Revelation's context, the obvious referent would have been Rome. The many transgressions of this woman mean, in the eyes of Revelation's writer, that she "deserves" abuse and exploitation. Revelation 17:16 reads, "And the ten horns that you saw, they and the beast will hate the whore; they will make her desolate and naked; they will devour her flesh and burn her up with fire."

This is not a neutral passage for those who have survived sexualized violence, or who love survivors. While many interpreters have avoided dealing with the sexualized violence in these passages or dealt with it indirectly, the ability to walk away from the violence in this text is a privilege that many do not have. Specifically, because the New Testament has so often been seen as a safe place (especially in contrast to the violence of the Old Testament), the presence of sexualized violence in these final passages can be a nasty surprise. And even more particularly because these passages involve Jesus Christ (who is the one throwing Jezebel on the bed in Revelation 2!), this imagery can become all the more painful.

Can the promises of Revelation, that Jesus is ushering in "a new heaven and a new earth" (Revelation 21:1), really be true if there's still sexualized violence in the fresh creation? To me, a new heaven and a new earth that still has sexualized violence feels much too close to the old world to be much good for survivors. The use of sexualized violence as a justified retribution bespeaks a victim-blaming view of sexualized violence that, I believe, will never stand up to the grace and love of God. No matter what we have done, no matter what our enemies (whomever they may be) have done, sexualized violence is not an acceptable punishment.

So why does this kind of violent imagery mar what's supposed to be the beautiful culmination of the New Testament, the grand, triumphant finale of Jesus Christ's ultimate reign over all the earth? Well, if we go back to the beginning of Revelation, we can remember that it is a vision, a dream of John during his imprisonment on the island of Patmos. And sometimes that dream is *strange*. Written in the apocalypse genre, which frequently uses bizarre imagery that signifies a coded message to an audience in the know, the writer is trying to use shocking images that will jar his audience out of complacency into a new commitment to the realization of God's reign.

This dream does not need to be our dream. The realization of God's kingdom that we can dream from a deep commitment to survivors' experiences cannot be one that is marred by the nightmare of rape. The Jesus whom we love and follow cannot engage in sexualized, violent behaviors as a sign of his reign. In moments in the text like these, which threaten to tear apart our faith in the goodness of God and the possibility of our discipleship, I believe we have to recognize how diversely the Bible actually speaks. *Dramatically* different images of Jesus come to us even within the New Testament itself.

And some of these images of Jesus do much to challenge the violent one we find in Revelation of Jesus throwing a woman on a bed or the "Jezebel" becoming subject to abuse. The abuse of power that becomes apparent in these texts is a power that Jesus has set aside and rejected. For me, the text of Philippians 2 reflects the kind of power that Jesus' reign encompasses.

> Let the same mind be in you that was in Christ Jesus,
> who, though he was in the form of God,
> > did not regard equality with God
> > as something to be exploited,
> but emptied himself,
> > taking the form of a slave,
> > being born in human likeness.
> And being found in human form,
> > he humbled himself
> > and became obedient to the point of death—
> > even death on a cross.
> (Philippians 2:5-8)

Jesus' very identity stands against the way that sexualized violence exploits power. While sexualized violence involves an unjust power grab, Jesus' display of power is a relinquishment of his privilege in favor of a sharing in our vulnerability. This is what the Greek word *kenosis* refers to: an utter emptying of Jesus' divinity into our humanity. The power that Jesus does have is one in which we can trust, because we have witnessed his *kenosis*. It's a different kind of power altogether from the exploitative power that victimizes us. It's a power that gives *us* power by stating that we are all part of the body of Christ. Here is how Philippians characterizes the power that Jesus does have:

> Therefore God also highly exalted him
> > and gave him the name

that is above every name,
so that at the name of Jesus
    every knee should bend,
        in heaven and on earth and under the earth,
and every tongue should confess
    that Jesus Christ is Lord,
to the glory of God the Father.
(Philippians 2:9-11)

The power that Jesus holds is a power that he holds along-side his servanthood. Jesus does not achieve power over us in ways that exploit and abuse us. Jesus' power is one that comes from his willingness to relinquish his power for us. Jesus' enthronement and exaltation in these verses of Philippians comes *after* the part about Jesus' rejection of "power over" in the traditional senses of the word.

For those of us who have become accustomed to experiencing power in abusive ways, this aspect of Jesus' lordship is crucial. We could not trust a Jesus who uses his power to manipulate us, coerce us, or otherwise harm us. But the power made manifest in Jesus Christ is, I believe, a power that can become trustworthy for survivors of sexualized violence. We can trust a Christ who, sharing in divine nature, renounced his privilege to be born to poor parents and narrowly escape genocide. We can trust a Christ whose power to work super-natural miracles uplifts the least of these. We can trust a Christ who has experienced, alongside us, so much of the human experience—including experiencing the trauma of sexual-ized violence.

All of this means that, for me, the image in Revelation of Jesus' participation in the sexual abuse of women who deserve "punishment" is profoundly out of character with the Jesus Christ revealed in Scripture. We have to remind ourselves that

Scripture does not speak in one voice. The witness of Scripture is not always consistent across different books of the Bible. This, to me, is because God revealed himself in different ways to different human authors of Scripture—and sometimes, these authors missed the mark. The norms of their times and their own lived experiences limited the authors' ability to reflect the fullness of God's vision for creation. You and I are much the same. Where in one area we may have far-sighted vision and an insightful sense of God's voice to us, at other times we may fall far short of the goodness and love that God extends to the whole world.

So these moments in Revelation that depict the consummation of Jesus' kingship as taking place through sexualized, violent acts are those that we may need to set aside in favor of the many other images of Scripture that show Jesus' solidarity and mercy toward those who have experienced sexualized violence. Scripture, sometimes internally inconsistent, can witness to *itself* at the points where the human authors fall short of showing God's abundant grace. The many texts in the New Testament that model how Jesus chooses nonviolent and life-affirming means to exercise his divine power witness *against* the suggestion in Revelation that sexualized violence could be part of Jesus' reign.

What are we supposed to do, then, when we encounter these violent passages in Revelation? I think it's a helpful wake-up call. Christians often have the anti-Jewish idea that *our* part of the Bible is exempt from the charges of violence that assail the Old Testament. This simply is not true. The New Testament has its own forms of violence. When we encounter these, as we do in Revelation, we need to grapple with them. Choosing to either ignore this violence or simply throw out the text lets us off the hook and avoids the real problem, however: these

violent passages are in our sacred texts, and like it or not, we
have to find a way to deal with them.

It can be possible for us to accept the message the author
is trying to convey but reject the means the author uses to
take us there. In the case of the "whore of Babylon" and the
"Jezebel" in Revelation, we may well need to reject the violent imagery that's being used. Reading through a lens that
seeks to be survivor-centered, the use of women in this way is
unacceptable. The Bible constitutes part of culture and forms
culture even as culture forms how we read the Bible. Letting
violent images such as these pass without our comment signals
our tacit approval of letting them continue to feed our imagi-
nations of what women "deserve" to experience.

However, though this violent imagery is something we may
choose to reject, the message behind it is perhaps one that we
can begin to unpack and unpeel. The message of Revelation is
unapologetically anti-imperialist. Revelation's message is that
contrary to all appearances, the biggest empires on the world
stage aren't supremely powerful. They are not God. They too
will fall apart when Jesus comes to reign. The shocking language of sexualized violence helps the author, writing in his
own context, further this anti-imperial agenda. Its violence
reflects the violence of the empires against which it speaks.
The author is still accountable for the violence in the text.
It *does* mean, however, that the violence in the text can be
read as reenacting the violence that Jews and early Christians
experienced, at times, at the hands of Rome.

We know that in situations of occupation and conflict, sexualized violence happens tragically often. The Bible itself bears
witness to how violence manifests in so many different ways
during warfare and occupation. Lamentations, which is one
of the most extended and graphic depictions of conflict in the

Bible, refers often to sexualized violence as it describes how enemies, acting, the writers feel, with the consent or at least inaction of God, rape the women of Jerusalem. But we don't need to go to ancient history to realize this; we can look around our own world to innumerable situations of conflict to see how sexualized violence is so often used as a weapon of warfare. As a young teenager, I was shocked by the images of abuse that I saw coming from my country's own prison camps. Members of the armed forces used sexualized violence against supposed enemy combatants as a form of humiliation and intimidation. Rape and abuse send a host of messages to an occupied people. It tells those who are raped that the occupier controls their bodies and minds absolutely. It tells women that they are the property of men. It tells men that they are no better than women. It tells mothers and fathers that they cannot protect their children. It tells an entire people that its lineage can be wiped out by a generation of involuntary pregnancies. I believe that the Jewish communities under Roman occupation experienced this as well, as recent scholarship has suggested that sexualized intimidation took place under the Roman regime.[2]

When a people group faces trauma like that, experienced through sexualized violence as well as manifold other crimes of warfare and oppressions, sometimes the only words left within us are violent words as well. The only language present to utter the complete outrage of what we have experienced are words of anger and hurt. In John's apocalyptic vision, the generational trauma that he has experienced as part of Roman occupation manifests itself as he describes violent and sexualized acts happening to women who represent hostile foreign powers.

But the whole of Revelation is not violent. There are beautiful, moving images of what the world will be like under the fullness of Christ's reign. These images are utterly incommensurate with the sexualized violence pictured in Revelation. This is possible because, in Revelation 20, "the dragon, that ancient serpent, who is the Devil and Satan," is locked up and thrown into a pit. The final victory is won.

The presence of evil in the world takes many forms. Earlier in my life, I was loathe to ascribe the language of "the devil" or "Satan" to this presence of evil. But to channel our anger productively, I think we sometimes need evil to have a face. And that face should not be the face of our neighbors (who often become the scapegoats of our own insecurities and pain), but the face of an evil much deeper, much more ultimate. So these days, I don't have much trouble with calling that ultimate evil Satan. Revelation speaks of that evil being banished forever under Jesus' reign. Taking shape as a dragon, Satan is imprisoned because of his incommensurability with the beautiful and peaceful reign of God: "Then I saw an angel coming down from heaven, holding in his hand the key to the bottomless pit and a great chain. He seized the dragon, that ancient serpent, who is the Devil and Satan, and bound him for a thousand years" (Revelation 20:1-2). Unfortunately, Satan's imprisonment is not permanent, and he gets a temporary reprieve from his imprisonment as he is allowed to emerge for just a little while to bring about the doom of the nations who threaten Christ's reign. Ultimately, Satan meets his final demise in the lake of fire during the final battle in Revelation (v. 10).

Jesus' reign will mean the final defeat of all the evil in the world that holds us captive. Sin and death will be no more. Revelation demonstrates that these powers, as formidable and terrifying as they are as we encounter them in this imperfect life, are not ultimate. Jesus is king over them. Jesus, the peaceful warrior, has come to defeat them. In his resurrection, we see the end result of this victory, as the grave cannot hold Jesus. But we're still living in the working out of this great victory. We still experience sin, pain, and death. We still live in a world that falls far short of God's wildest, most beautiful dreams.

For survivors, sexualized violence is a huge part of their encounter with this ultimate evil. We experience the hold of Satan's power when we are told, through forceful word and action, that our bodies are not created in the image of God, are not temples of the Holy Spirit, worthy of respect and care. We experience the hold of Satan's power when we are told that our testimonies are false and that whatever we have experienced is our own fault. We experience the hold of Satan's power when our lives feel defined by the worst things that have ever happened to us.

The hope announced in Revelation is that the totality of evil we experience will not have a hold on us anymore. Even sexualized violence, which has played such a commanding and destructive role in many people's narratives, can be destroyed. The holy fire of Jesus' reign, destroying every oppression, will obliterate the hold that rape, abuse, incest, exploitation, and every other form of sexualized violence have on us.

What will remain is God's perfect peace. We will be able to witness creation restored and renewed. The struggle and hurt from our past will come into a totally new perspective as we behold the goodness that Jesus brings with his reign. The turmoil described earlier in Revelation will give way to God's perfect peace. As John narrates this transition, we can see the change that takes place from the chaos of conflict earlier in Revelation to a transformed world: "Then I saw a new heaven and a new earth; for the first heaven and the first earth had passed away, and the sea was no more. And I saw the holy city, the new Jerusalem, coming down out of heaven from God, prepared as a bride adorned for her husband" (Revelation 21:1-2).

This beautiful image here of a totally reimagined creation, a place where God's peaceful, comforting presence is fully felt and experienced, is an image that, perhaps, resonates with the deepest longings of our hearts. This image jars with the earlier violence in Revelation, and ultimately, I believe the two are incompatible. A Christ whose reign is one of peace and justice cannot cement his rule through sexualized violence. Nor could we justifiably worship a god (lowercase *g* intentional here) whose rule created this unjust, power-based suffering. Revelation also challenges readers conscious of the dynamics of sexualized violence through its use of the bride of Christ metaphor for the church, recalling the marital imagery of the Hebrew Prophets. However, the bride of Christ imagery also presents an opportunity for transforming what marriage and intimacy would mean in Christ's reign. We can begin to imagine a reality in which marriage and intimacy truly reflect a Christlike relationship with power and the divine goodness in one another. Understanding sexuality as a self-giving yet self-affirming embrace of one another, we could truly bring our whole selves—safely and powerfully—into communion with God and others.

That truly will be a mark of Christ's reign.

RETRACING
THE JOURNEY

I've said a lot of things in this book. Some of them you may agree with. Some of them you probably disagree with. But I hope, more than anything else, this book made you think about things in our Scripture and in our world, and how the two intersect with each other. My prayer is that aspects of what I've talked about, even if not my words themselves, have given life, strength, and hope to you on your journey, whether you are a survivor, a minister, or someone who is hoping to learn more about how to read the Bible and support survivors in the communities that you love.

Of all the points that I've made in this book, I think a few are especially central and important. I'll list those here:

1. God stands in solidarity with those who are suffering. We can trust that God is with us when we experience sexualized violence and its aftermath, and that God is still contending for our wholeness. If no one else in the world can hear our testimony, God hears us, and God is working out justice, no matter how deep the brokenness we feel. Oftentimes, sexualized violence intersects with other types of oppressions to make the

forces against us seem even stronger. So the struggle in which God is engaging with us becomes even more critical as the fight against sexualized violence needs to join forces with allies working against racism, heterosexism, classism, xenophobia, and other ways in which people try to deny the image of God in one another.

The suffering we experience is known to God, too. The Christian affirmation that Jesus Christ is fully God and fully human and that Jesus experienced the scandal of the cross points to God's intimate knowledge of every aspect of our existence, including sexualized violence. In Christ, God has experienced what it is like to feel the full weight of our shame and pain—and to survive, even with scars. Jesus' life and ministry bears witness to what a life fully lived in solidarity with suffering looks like.

2. We should not be alone, void of human community. God created us for community. God has raised up leaders, healers, and other allies who can stand with us as we seek healing and wholeness in all parts of our lives. These people, gifts from God, represent the body of Christ in our lives as they remind us through their human presence of the goodness and faithfulness of God. For those in ministry with survivors, I am deeply grateful. I urge you, even as you seek to lead survivors toward greater healing and wholeness, to attend to your own wellness. Remember that the light you offer needs kindling too. Seek out spaces and times where you can experience the love and care you offer so often to others.

3. The stories of the Bible that touch on sexualized violence are often difficult and painful to read. These are not stories that are necessarily right to read in all times and places. There may be times when these stories are too triggering for survivors

and those who love them to read while foregrounding their own safety and well-being. Whenever these stories are read in community, trust must be built first. Their reading needs to be introduced with a content warning so that people are not blindsided by what's going on. There needs to be space for discussion, response, and often, lament.

There have been moments when I have pushed back against the way the Bible tells stories. There are times when I have suggested that the theology of the biblical writers is flawed. The Bible was not written with survivors in mind, especially. And often, the biases of the biblical writers—as well as the biases of their interpreters—come through. But despite the pain in the stories, despite their problems, I believe the biblical texts issue an invitation for us to stand in witness of trauma. There are moments where survivor voices are heard, however faintly, and moments when those who stand beside them appear as well. There are moments when pain and hope sit together, however uneasily. There are moments where we uncomfortably find our world reflected in the text, however much we'd like to remove ourselves from what we perceive as the "backwardness" of ancient times.

4. Scripture doesn't tell us how to think. It speaks in many different voices, from the fragmented but eloquent pain of Daughter Zion in Lamentations 1–2 to the profound silence of Dinah in Genesis 34. "God" is compared to everything from an abusive husband to a devoted mother. Sometimes the suffering that Scripture talks about seems to be linked to human failings; other times, it doesn't. We need to bring our eyes, ears, mind, and heart to engage Scripture, as well as those of our whole community. We need to discern the truth arising through Scripture using all of these tools.

And we also need to discern what is true using the revelation that is still coming to us. I think that if we really get in touch with what's going on deep inside of us, we can know that we are good, beloved, and God's. This truth needs to be at the forefront of everything we read in Scripture as we encounter the sometimes-confusing texts of sexualized violence within our Scriptures. If we lose sight of these truths, we can risk harm as we read Scripture. A God who called us good, beloved, and God's own does not will sexualized violence into our lives, no matter how confusing the Scriptures can be on the subject.

5. For survivors, I offer that, even with all the complexities of Scripture, even with all the pain represented within it and the pain it can conjure within us at times, we have the power to reclaim the Bible as a living Word in our lives. This is not at all an admonition to overlook how difficult it is for us to read parts of Scripture or to accept, unquestioningly, passages that seem to dehumanize us. Rather, I encourage you to hold on to what you know is true of yourself, God, and our world, and meanwhile remain in conversation with Scripture. As in Genesis 32, when Jacob wrestles with the angel, sometimes the blessing is found through struggle. Struggle in and of itself is not necessarily fun, yet I deeply believe that there is something beautiful, something healing, available within Scripture, if we are willing to sell what we have for that pearl of great price (Matthew 13:45-46).

* * *

Sexualized violence changes us. It harms us, yet through God's work even in the midst of terrible circumstances, we can heal, transform, and fulfill the wildest dreams that God has for our lives. Scripture witnesses over and over to the great harm of sexualized violence, and not every story has a happy ending. But Scripture also points to God's persistence in continuing to work in and among us even as humanity causes and experiences brokenness.

The story of God's work among his people is ongoing. The Spirit of God is still striving in you and in me, in our communities, in our world. Thank *goodness* the story of God's work isn't over yet, when so much sexualized violence still exists to harm us. There is hope for our future, even when the lights of truth, hope, and justice—the light of Christ—feel dim in the present. Scripture begins the story of God's miraculous presence and intervention, and it's still being written in our hearts each day.

As you, with the Spirit, continue your story, whether that is your story of being a survivor, an ally, or someone just trying to figure out what the Bible has to do with sexualized violence, I pray these blessings upon you:

May God bless you with the knowledge of how deeply and wholly you are loved.

May God bless you with the power to rage where rage is due.

May God bless you with compassion for others, even in your own struggle.

May God bless you with peace in the in-between times, before all is made right.

May God bless you with the sight of a world not yet realized.

May that future world be free of the brokenness we see now.

Amen.

RESOURCES
FOR SUPPORT

Rape, Abuse, and Incest National Network (RAINN)
https://www.rainn.org

National Sexual Assault Telephone Hotline
1-800-656-HOPE (1-800-656-4673)

VictimConnect Resource Center
https://victimconnect.org
chat.victimsofcrime.org
1-855-4VICTIM (1-855-484-2846)

Centers for Disease Control, Violence Prevention: Sexual Violence
https://www.cdc.gov/violenceprevention/sexualviolence/index.html

1 in 6 *(support for male survivors)*
https://1in6.org

Know Your IX: Empowering Students to Stop Sexual Violence
https://www.knowyourix.org

National Alliance on Mental Illness
https://www.nami.org

Into Account
https://intoaccount.org

Dove's Nest
https://dovesnest.net

Resources on Sexual Violence and the Church, Anabaptist Mennonite Biblical Seminary
https://libraryguides.ambs.edu/sexualviolence

NOTES

CHAPTER 1

1 For the sake of simplicity, I've opted to use the names Sarah and Abraham, given to Sarai and Abram in Genesis 17, for all discussion of their story in Genesis.

2 For a discussion of various interpretative possibilities for this verse, see, for example, Robert Alter, *The Hebrew Bible: A Translation with Commentary, The Prophets* (New York: W. W. Norton, 2019), 347.

CHAPTER 2

1 For a more detailed explanation of traumatic reenactment, see Michael S. Levy, "A Helpful Way to Conceptualize and Understand Reenactments," *Journal of Psychotherapy Practice and Research* 1998, 7:227–35, https://www.ncbi.nlm.nih.gov/pmc/articles/PMC3330499/.

2 Cori Doerrfeld, *The Rabbit Listened*, Dial Books for Young Readers (New York: Random House, 2018).

CHAPTER 3

1 "Intimate Partner Violence, Sexual Violence, and Stalking among Men," CDC, last reviewed June 1, 2020, https://www.cdc.gov/violenceprevention/datasources/nisvs/men-ipvsvandstalking.html.

2 For more on this interpretation of Lot's older daughter recruiting her sister to rape their father with her, see Matthew J. Korpman, "Can Anything Good Come from Sodom? A Feminist and Narrative Critique of Lot's Daughters in Genesis 19:30-38," *Journal for the Study of the Old Testament* 43, no. 3 (2019): 334–42.

3 Sarah Maslin Nir, "How Two Lives Collided in Central Park, Rattling the Nation," *New York Times*, June 14, 2020, https://www.nytimes.com/2020/06/14/nyregion/central-park-amy-cooper-christian-racism.html.

4 Susanne Scholz, *Sacred Witness: Rape in the Hebrew Bible* (Minneapolis: Augsburg Fortress Publishers, 2014).

CHAPTER 4

1 For a more detailed scholarly analysis of the social scientific understanding of fictive kinship and its role in the New Testament, see Abera M. Mengestu, *God as Father in Paul: Kinship Language and Identity Formation in Early Christianity* (Eugene, OR: Pickwick, 2013).

CHAPTER 5

1 A wonderful resource to explore the trauma histories behind Scripture is David M. Carr's book *Holy Resilience: The Bible's Traumatic Origins* (New Haven: Yale University Press, 2014).

CHAPTER 6

1 Rocío Figueroa and David Tombs have done pioneering work examining the crucifixion of Jesus as an instance of sexual abuse, including reading this story alongside the narratives of contemporary survivors. See, for example, Figueroa and Tombs, "Recognising Jesus as a Victim of Sexual Abuse," *Religion and Gender* 10, no. 1 (2020): 57–75.

2 See, for example, the important work of David Tombs on the role of sexual abuse in the Roman Empire. Tombs, "Crucifixion, State Terror, and Sexual Abuse: Text and Context," *Union Seminary Quarterly Review* 53 (Autumn 1999): 80–109, available at the Otago Research Archive, http://hdl.handle.net/10523/8558.

THE AUTHOR

Susannah Larry is assistant professor of biblical studies at Anabaptist Mennonite Biblical Seminary, where she brings together academic rigor and deep faith commitments. She is passionate about helping churches think about how to make space for their congregants to process grief through lament and about reflecting on women in  the Bible. She holds a PhD in Hebrew Bible and ancient Israel from Vanderbilt University. Though she was denominationally nomadic for several years, Susannah now feels at home in Anabaptist and Mennonite traditions and attends Hively Avenue Mennonite Church in Elkhart, Indiana. She blogs at SusannahMarieLarry.com.